W9-BNT-566

QUEENS OF THE RESISTANCE:
ELIZABETH WARREN

ALSO IN THE
QUEENS OF THE RESISTANCE SERIES

Alexandria Ocasio-Cortez
Nancy Pelosi
Maxine Waters

QUEENS
OF THE
RESISTANC

QUEENS OF THE RESISTANCE:

ELIZABETH WARREN

The Life, Times, and
Rise of Warren, aka the *Boss*

BRENDA JONES AND KRISHAN TROTMAN

PLUME

An imprint of Penguin Random House LLC
penguinrandomhouse.com

Illustrations by Jonell Joshua
Interior Hand Lettering by Jonell Joshua and Dominique Jones

LIBRARY OF CONGRESS CATALOGING-IN-PUBLICATION DATA
has been applied for.

ISBN 9780593189863 (POB)
ISBN 9780593189900 (ebook)

Printed in the United States of America
1 3 5 7 9 10 8 6 4 2

BOOK DESIGN BY TIFFANY ESTREICHER

For Elizabeth Warren,
and all the Queens of the Resistance reading this

CONTENTS

III. LEADER

IV. RESISTANCE

V. QUEEN

You wanna be this Queen B,
But ya can't be
That's why you're mad at me.
—Lil' Kim, "Big Momma Thang"

INTRODUCTION: THE QUEENS OF THE RESISTANCE SERIES

Dear Sis,

The Queens of the Resistance is a series that celebrates the life and times as well as the lessons and rise of our favorite sheroes and Queen Bees of politics. It's a celebration of the *boss,* the loud in their demands, and a rebellion against the long and tired patriarchy. They are the shining light and new face of the US government. The idea for the series began to germinate in 2016. Hillary Clinton was in the presidential race. She was top dog, Grade A. She was supposed to go all the way as the first female president. She had done everything right. In the 1960s, she switched parties when the Civil Rights movement was demonstrating that changing allegiance wasn't about betting on the winner but believing in a different vision for America's future. She married one of the most capable politicians of the twentieth century, Bill Clinton, who would eventually appoint the first Black secretaries of commerce and labor and put women and minorities in many positions of power. She was considered most likely to be president when she gave a commencement speech during her graduation from Wellesley, then went on to graduate Yale Law at the head of her class. She was the first female partner of two law firms in Arkansas; First Lady of Arkansas; First Lady of the United States—but she didn't stop there. She became the first female US senator from New York, a seat that had positioned Robert Kennedy to run for president, and one of the first female secretaries of state. She was the first woman *ever* to be nominated by a major political party to run for president. Even the political machine was oiled and greased to work in her favor. She had been generally considered one of the most qualified people ever to run for president, even by her opponents, but with all that going for her, somehow, some way, she didn't make it. **sigh** You can't get more presidential than Hillary Clinton in 2016. She had it all, even the majority of popular votes in the 2016 election.

So what happened? Ha! Every woman knows what happened! Everybody laughed at her in 1995, when she appeared on the *Today* show and attributed the chop-down of her husband to a "vast right-wing conspiracy," but she was right. Who knew that while we were enjoying the moment, the wind beneath our wings after two terms with the first Black president, a time that had left us proximal to a variety of enjoyable mini multi-cultures—sushi, guacamole, break dancing—there was a group of malcontents intent on making America great again . . . "great" like the 1940s. And that meant forcing women back into the kitchen, padlocking the door, and throwing away the key. There'd be no need to vilify female candidates with memes, negative ads, and sucker punches like the opposition had to do to Hillary Clinton; the social stigma would do all the policing and policy work needed to keep women out of the ring and out of the way, so the boyz could rule, unchecked, unaccountable, and unrestrained. "Less for you, more for me" has been a natural law in a capitalist society. It means getting rid of competition by every means necessary—deportation, mass incarceration, legislation, deprivation, deconstruction, and divestment, to name a few. Our sister Hillary was a woman who fell in the crosshairs of a right-wing machine dead set against any diversion from its outrageous plan—to stop collective action and make sure politics bends only to its will, not the people's. It didn't matter that Hillary was the smartest, the most prepared, or the first in this or that. Merit's not the point; it's compliance that matters, and Hillary was just too damn smart, too capable, too talented, for her own good. She had a vast right-wing conspiracy working against her, and they won . . . temporarily.

And that's where this series begins. Queens of the Resistance is as much an ode to the women themselves as it is a celebration of a transcending political identity in America, unlike anything our history has ever shown us before.

With Love,
Brenda & Krishan

QUEENS OF THE RESISTANCE:
ELIZABETH WARREN

★ ★ ★ ★ ★ ★ ★ ★ ★ ★ ★

BORN

My name is Elizabeth, and I'm running for president because that's what girls do.

—ELIZABETH WARREN

THE TAO OF BETSY

I promise that you'll never find another like me.

—Taylor Swift, "ME!"

Elizabeth Warren is a five-foot-eight *boss*, a woman who starts the fight and wins it, an indisputable Queen of the Resistance. She has led the battle for the middle class since the 1960s. Warren has a plan, and she persists, honey. *Snap. Snap*—that's just how she rolls. She's a political samurai and will go after a meaningful cause like a bulldog after a bone. In any race or debate, she is a top contender. The Warren jogs out to the podium, appearing unassuming in a soft-knit, crayon-blue blazer and rimless glasses, but then suddenly she's throwing blows like Muhammad Ali—at rich politicians attempting to buy the presidency, big banks, and Wall Street, or men trying to dictate women's choices. Warren comes to *slay* and annihilate these dirty tricksters. She's also equally as excited to learn, eager to educate, and wants to touch the beating heart of the American people. But don't be fooled by this skinny little girl from Norman, Oklahoma. Warren can land a swing, like Balboa, to get her point across, and delivers politics for the knockout: facts, analysis, what's right not wrong for your nana's healthcare in West Palm Beach. She'll work you through an economics report with the skill and precision of a surgeon. *Trump, beware.* She's done the research, got the blueprints, and will undo you.

What makes her a feared opponent is her willingness to drill down to the facts in a way that only yo mama could do. Her research is deep and wide, and, trust me, she's got *receipts*. She'll *read* you on financial law and equity with such deep affection it'll sound like a romance novel. Your mind will be opened, you will see a new vision of what life could be in America. And she's effective, this force is a political heavyweight!

Just when you thought the "good guys" were dead—you know, the good guys who hurry in on white horses kicking up a cloud of dust ready to save the day? The same white men we see over and over again coming to the rescue—Thor, the Hulk, and Iron Man types, rockin' configurations of the Avengers, gathering their powers, ready to pounce back the forces of evil in a big showdown one more time? When the skies are particularly cloudy, and you find yourself mad at the universe, sick of the ongoing media headlines and news announcing a corrupt president has gotten off the hook yet again—including a 448-page report that suggests reason for impeachment—and you're wondering whether the proverbial good guys are tired, whipped, and tucked in bed, then you might take a long, hard, very serious look at Elizabeth Warren. She's no good guy; she's the best woman!

While most of us are lost in deep meditative thought, picking our noses or sipping our merlot trying to figure out why our hard work can't seem to put us ahead, Elizabeth "Betsy" Warren has been investigating those same questions for us and configuring answers about what happened to the American dream for the last forty years. And she's also been trying to do something about it for the last forty years. . . . That sort of tenacity, bullish spirit, supernatural *slay* power makes you realize the good ol' guys coming to the rescue just might be the gals.

She has been listening in to American life like a studious internist for decades, to find causes and effects, to gather data, draw conclusions, and develop her own form of quantitative easing. She's taken the stethoscope of her mind and carefully examined the American chest, its labored breathing, its sputtering and wheezing. She has been sounding the alarm, trying to tell us in her own professorial way how to fix our systems, and why all that's wrong might not be our fault. Warren's no diva, no duchess wannabe. There's no airs about Warren. She'd chug a beer before sipping wine. She's busy. There's work to be done and this queen is determined to do it.

So where did this Queen of the Resistance come from?

* * *

SHE'S BETSY HERRING. That's what her mama called her. Her daddy was Don Herring and her mother was born Pauline "Polly" Reed. Her parents grew up in a small town in Wetumka, Oklahoma. Her daddy's family owned a hardware store. After some difficulties in the family—more on that in a moment—Don wore many hats: he sold cars, fixed fences, and worked as a salesman at Montgomery Ward department store in the rug section. After the war, he and Pauline moved from place to place, one step ahead of the next bill collector and to wherever Don could find work.

The Herrings had three boys, Don, John, and David . . . and when their sons were all nearly grown and about to leave home, in the summer of 1949, surprise, surprise! Baby Betsy was born on June 22, a Cancer—creative, thoughtful, emotional, and highly loyal and empathetic to others, according to the stars. Betsy's daddy dubbed her the whipped cream with "the cherry on top." Polly was thirty-seven, and had thought her childbirth days were over, but finally she got a girl. A girl she'd adorn with pink bows, sparkles, and red shoes. Hooray!

(Feminists, hush. Betsy would eventually put gender stereotypes on blast in her politics.)

Still, the Herrings were considered a middle-class family, and a surprise baby bundle of joy wasn't a threat to their livelihood. Despite the challenges he faced, Betsy's father was an idealist, dedicated to the dream of becoming the emblem of the American suburban family: two parents and a few kids, living on one income—her father's, of course. Her mother readily embraced the role of stay-at-home mom, which was typical at that time, *otay*. They owned a home in Norman, twenty miles south of Oklahoma City. The Herrings were no replica of *The Truman Show* or *Stepford Wives*. They were not rich, but for years they managed to hack it as homeowners and were considered middle-class; they had a stable footing with the seeds they'd planted. Her parents were able to buy their home with the help of a federal loan—Americans back then didn't need to be millionaires to succeed. Looking back at that time, Elizabeth Warren often remembers it fondly—sort of wistfully, like an Alice who had seen the magical flowers of Wonderland yet somehow they'd withered away.

But the stability she'd felt at home while growing up was not to last.

In fact, it would briskly be pulled from under her in what felt like the blink of an eye, leaving a feeling that seeps at the feet of a terrible coming.

"YES, MISS BETSY, YOU CAN!"

I know I can be what I wanna be.

—Nas, "I Know I Can"

It was Elizabeth's second-grade teacher, Mrs. Lee, who first told her that she could in fact, "*do something.*"

It was the 1950s, and women like Mrs. Lee were a mystery, a puzzle. She was "a woman with sturdy shoes, an ample bosom, and a surprisingly gravelly voice," as Warren described in her book *This Fight Is Our Fight*. But she was an enigma to young Betsy coming of age in a world where the worth of a woman was judged by how well she kept her home, the neatness of her children's appearance, her award-winning casseroles, and the longevity of her marriage. Some women had worked in factories during the war, but working was still largely considered a mandatory drudgery for single women, a penance for those who somehow missed the memo on how to get and keep a man—it was *not* a life to aspire to, Beyoncé.

Being a housewife was the everyday luxury for neighborhood wives with respect and social standing. It was supposed to be the goal of every little girl. This would become a concern for Betsy, fellow A-cups, and any tomboy who dared to show her true colors. Early on, Betsy knew that she did not have all the requisite requirements—sizing herself up in the mirror, a stark assessment made it clear she was not a Betty Grable or Marilyn Monroe. Somewhere in her heart, she wanted to be some guy's great catch too, but she felt her most compelling characteristic was her brain. And her mother didn't help, Warren said. "She fretted that I didn't do 'normal girl things' like trying on makeup or curling my hair, and she used to remind me not to wear my reading glasses."

But second-grade Betsy was fond of Mrs. Lee, who seemed to cast spells that made math fun, reading joyful, and her classroom a magical place to be. Mrs. Lee led the class with grace and brilliance and gifted her students with both "smoky hugs" and a command for order. She challenged Betsy to think differently about who she was and fostered an environment where even a girl could "*do something.*"

Betsy told Mrs. Lee that she'd become a teacher just like her when she grew up. She was one of the best readers in class, so Mrs. Lee put Betsy in charge of a reading group to help other students. There, she relished the power of teaching—the thrill it granted of watching her peers advance—and that role continued on to the playground, where Betsy would shepherd other second graders into her imaginary classroom. She'd work her teaching magic at home too, where she'd hold rousing lectures in her bedroom for her dolls and teddy bears.

Mrs. Lee had created a North Star for Betsy, where the loftiest path a girl from the suburbs of Norman, Oklahoma, was supposed to take was to marry a boy. And though Betsy would sometimes lose sight of that star, Mrs. Lee's allure had already planted an uncommon seed in her mind: she could "*do something*." This new philosophy, this indestructible understanding would serve as a guide to Betsy for the rest of her life. She could be a badass, if she chose to.

It was in the halls of Wilson Elementary School with Mrs. Lee where she first learned that being "different" was not a handicap but her greatest power, and this new understanding elevated her out of mediocrity into a place of superiority. "I had [absorbed] the message that I was a pretty iffy case—not very pretty, not very flirty, and definitely not very good at making boys feel like they were smarter than I was." Education would be her big escape. Even at a young age, Betsy knew there was something gnawing at the center of her life, and it was sometimes painfully clear that she would never be the woman her mother had raised her to be. There is no way her parents could have known that America had turned a corner, that opportunities for women would abound for almost fifty years, that women would break through a glass ceiling that Pauline never even desired to see through, let

A FIGHTER IS BORN

alone bust out of, but change was coming. In fact, this movement had already begun, and Betsy Herring would one day reign as a Queen of the Resistance.

Young Betsy knew that education would be a driving force, a veritable race car ride out of Norman, Oklahoma. An education is a meal ticket, as Malcolm X said: "Education is our passport to the future, for tomorrow belongs only to the people who prepare for it today." In fact, education has been the primary mover toward change for women and people of color throughout history. In the 1950s and '60s, while Betsy was growing up after World War II, the government funneled money into colleges and universities to help veterans returning home. Student loans and grants were made available to them and billions of dollars were poured into secondary schools for their education. This empowered Betsy's education and those of many middle-class families around the country. By the 1970s, when Betsy was seeking higher education, her commuter college was only $50 per semester. Education would become a huge part of her political agenda. She would continue to remember Mrs. Lee for years to come, especially as a member of the Senate education committee. But for now, she was just a little girl with a dream . . .

UNBREAKABLE

Life without dreaming is a life without meaning.

—Wale, "Aston Martin Music"

Things changed at home when Betsy's father had a heart attack. Sis, this is when the sand quickens, and a child's innocence begins to fog and is traded for awareness. Everyone has these moments when there's a hushed rumbling and the Earth slightly tilts, and things will never be the same. For Betsy it was when she was about to finish grade school. That day, her father had slid into a kitchen table chair, sunken and exhausted. Her mother called out for him to get up a few times but he couldn't. When they finally went to the hospital, the prognosis was clear. Betsy's father would survive, but he would never be quite the same. And neither would Elizabeth Warren.

In order to understand the heart of Elizabeth Warren, we must dive even deeper into the roots of where she comes from.

By the time they had Betsy, Don and Pauline Herring had

survived just about every kind of disaster: ecological retribution, capitalism run amok, the complete breakdown of the world financial system, world war, and the threat of nuclear holocaust. Despite disaster moving at a glacial pace or at top speed, like the katana-wielding, zombie-killing Michonne in *The Walking Dead*, the Herrings always stayed resilient and never stopped fighting for a better life—a fight Betsy would one day take up for all Americans.

They were just twenty-one and nineteen years old, it was 1932 in Wetumka, Oklahoma, when Don and Pauline decided to elope, to the consternation of their parents—especially Don's, who disapproved of Pauline's family background. The conflict over his new bride ultimately cost Don his relationship with his parents, and with it the livelihood that the family store could provide. Still, they were young and in love, not totally oblivious to the ramifications of the Great Depression but full of youthful optimism that recovery was just around the corner. The couple took a hopeful leap together into the future.

Don and Pauline had dreams of their own. Elizabeth remembers family lore being populated with stories of Don, barely out of high school and rebuilding a two-passenger, open-cockpit airplane. Then somehow he taught himself how to fly. It was the time of the wizardry of the Wright brothers and the technological miracle of flight when a fearless Don would meander in circles over and over again in the turquoise sky high over roving fields of wheat that spread like a golden band across the Oklahoma horizon. His favorite girl, Pauline, was bright, engaging, and could sing like an angel. In fact, she could get lost in song for hours, absorbed in melody and lyrics of starlit moonbeams and romantic reverie.

They had the warmth and snuggly comfort of love, but the Great Depression would last until Don and Pauline had nearly raised their entire family. Their marriage was ultimately their only anchor through enormous crises. Through food shortages, a lack of jobs, and mountains of unpaid bills. In Wetumka there were farms, and people who sewed their own clothes and lived in the same homes for decades, even generations. Places like Wetumka had been the saving grace of European immigrants, freed African Americans fleeing the South after the Civil War, and people from the eastern United States who were encouraged decades before to go west. At that time the federal government had offered huge tracts of land, from 160 to as many as 640 acres in some places, per family to settle new western territories it had purchased or won through the spoils of war. Don's and Pauline's parents or grandparents had likely been among some of those settlers who went west to follow their dreams. And when they got to Oklahoma in the late 1800s and early 1900s, it was lush farmland.

All throughout Don's and Pauline's childhoods, the fruits of the Great Plains were harvested and fed to the rest of the nation. For decades, settlers used newfangled machines to till the ground mechanically, digging deep into the soil, clearing it of all its roots and leaving a thick layer of topsoil that yielded harvests and plenty. But the settlers did not realize something the original native peoples who had lived there for centuries could have told them if they had only asked: the region was also prone to serious drought. At almost the same time that the couple was enjoying the bliss of their marriage and children, the sun began baking the soil and the clouds gave way to a boiling heat. The rain dried up and the soil turned to dust. All the beautiful, rich topsoil that had been so assiduously unearthed from the bedrock of the land by manmade, highly efficient, mechanical marvels suddenly became a weapon turned against them. Now industrialized but with no trees, no grasses, no mountains to brace against the whistling winds, huge clouds of unmoored dust began to push across the Midwest. No matter how well Don and Pauline sealed their home, once those high winds started to blow, somehow dust always seeped in through cracks in the doors and windows, ceilings and walls. Livestock were killed, and cars were buried in dunes of dirt. Meticulously plowed fields were dumped with mountains of sand, ruined for any future production. In 1934, just two years after the Herrings were married, and five years after the shortages of the Great Depression had begun, 300 million tons of dust blew from parts of Oklahoma and Texas all the way over to the Atlantic coast. By 1935, 850 million tons of dust blew through 101 counties in the country. That year there were forty-one dust storms, and in 1938, the worst year on record in Oklahoma, there were sixty-one. Consequently, mortgages failed at a rate of $25 million a day in mid-twentieth-century terms, equal to $450 million a day today.

These are *The Grapes of Wrath* that John Steinbeck built his classic novel around. His book told the story of people Don and Pauline might have known, and this is from whence the blood of Warren cometh.

BY THE TIME World War II came around, there had been shortages of bread, coffee, milk, gasoline, and so on, and folks had been living without for over a decade. (Pause: Some of you are stuck on the thought of living without coffee or bread for a decade. Yep, it was a tough time.) The Herrings, and most families, had scraping the bottom of the barrel down to a well-defined, very intricate science. There were war posters put up everywhere with instructions: "Food Is a Weapon. Don't Waste It." Or "Buy Wisely. Cook Carefully. Eat It All." Or "When You Ride Alone You Ride with Hitler . . . Join a Car Sharing Club." The speed limit was reduced to thirty-five miles per hour to conserve precious gasoline.

However, the war led to an additional organizing principle at the feet of the Great Depression. Big Brother became like a giant, cuddly friend who offered practical leadership at a time when Adolf Hitler, a vicious boogeyman who so neatly symbolized absolute evil and destruction, was hell-bent on conquering the world. There were finally jobs available, mainly for young men as soldiers and for young women as nurses and assistants for the Red Cross. Don hoped he might fulfill his longing to fly, but alas his hopes were dashed. He was hired by the Army Air Forces to be a flight instructor, not a pilot. So the Herrings moved about seventy-five miles north to Muskogee, where the military bases were.

After the war, Don still wanted to fly one of those big commercial jets for TWA (then Trans World Airlines). It was the heyday of airline travel, when flying was considered stylish, chic, and sophisticated. (Nowadays it's sweatpants and a little pillow drool.)

But alas, middle-aged now, Don was rejected again, deemed too old for that work. Heck, sis, he was competing with all the young war pilots who had earned their wings under the threat of world annihilation.

Soon enough the couple decided to move back home once more to Wetumka. Don's next venture was car repair, and he scraped together enough money with one of his homies to start a shop. He could fix anything, and his friend would manage the sales. The timing was perfect. Their repair shop would have just preceded the glory days of the American automobile, and it could have been a pathway out of struggle for the Herrings. The bad news is, Don's friend tapped out, took the money from the business, and ran. In the wake of the Great

Depression, the high hopes of success had kindled and built a bonfire that forged the emergence of the American middle class. Don's dreams had been dashed against the rocks, blown to smithereens by the deceit of an unjust world, and whisked away, insignificantly lost across the Oklahoma plains. But, like many hardworking Americans, he found work where he could and the family survived.

IT WAS SURVIVING the consequences of Don's poor health that the Herrings weren't as sure of.

After a time, Don tried to go back to the job he had at Montgomery Ward, but they had given it away to someone else. Betsy's mom told her it was because his manager assumed he was going to die. WTH?!

Doctors may have said it was the rich food that led to his chest pain, but it could have been that blood had stopped circulating through veins that had sustained years of hard work and strife. It could have been the strenuous bulking up only to be knocked down again. It could have been the weight of carrying an entire family on his shoulders, a labor of love that had held his life together by threads of affection but was not enough to keep his body going forever.

Given up for dead by a world he had fought so hard to live in, Don took another post at the store, but there was no salary attached. The work was on commission only. And finances became another uphill battle for the Herring family that amounted to a devastating loss of security.

Since the US healthcare system didn't work for families like theirs, Betsy and her mother had to make sacrifices. Chronic, debilitating illness is the sword that hangs over the livelihood of almost every American, except the super-rich. Even they, however, often leave American shores for places like Mexico and Switzerland, where they can get more advanced, less expensive medical treatments because other Western nations actually resolved their healthcare system issues a long time ago.

Betsy was twelve years old when she caught her mother crying in wobbly heels and a dress that fit too tightly. Facing destitution when her husband's medical bills piled up and his income dropped off so sharply, Mama Pauline was headed down to Sears to get a job. There, she got a position selling appliances, clothing, and home goods. At the snap of a finger, suddenly the stay-at-home mom was the breadwinner and anchor of the family, and she saved them from drowning in debt.

But it wasn't a total victory—Pauline never wanted to be that hero. Sis, this is not a Hollywood story à la Greta Gerwig where the heroine is whisked into Gloria Steinem–esque superpowers—no matter how much we wish that could be all of our stories. No, the truth is, girlfriend, there were a lot of tears. Probably the kind of tears cried silently in the closet or bathroom shielded away from the kids, but Betsy saw how painful it was for her mama bear. To Pauline, it was a dire sacrifice, devastating, and just freakin' tragic! "My mother was suspicious [toward] women who had families and worked," Warren wrote. "Working was for women who weren't lucky enough to have a husband and children." Pauline was fifty years old. It was a minimum-wage job. (Honey, a minimum-wage job at Sears supporting a family of six and a mortgage? That's almost unheard-of nowadays! But we'll get to that later.)

There was no reason to stomp, applaud, and break out the pussyhats for some of the women in Pauline's generation entering the workforce. Betsy's experience watching her mother go to work for the first time in her fifties is a story different from our own, where women are working and breaking the mold every day, whether in Gucci suits, pants and silk ties, or a good pair of Chuck Taylors while doing it. We're climbing out of our cribs with digital Rolodexes almost grafted to our spine. This generational shift lays bare how gender norms have drastically changed . . . and it's giving the patriarchy whiplash.

Still, as of 2017, 40 percent of mothers were the sole or primary breadwinners in their families. Pauline's story, however, would illustrate for Betsy and for all of us a great lesson in economics and would hold the seeds of a movement. This new way of life for American families—where the women, the Eves, the skirt-wearers and bra-bearers, are 50 percent of the population and work just as hard as men but earn less—is still outdated. Women are out of the home but 38 percent more likely than men to live in poverty. America's caretakers—the waitresses, cleaners, and home-care workers, for example—are predominantly women and make up two-thirds of minimum-wage workers, and their jobs often don't offer benefits. Women are graduating college at higher rates than men, and reaching the top of the salary chain less often. We're only 24 percent of Congress and 6 percent of Fortune 500 C-suite positions.

Pauline quickly came to understand the pain and triumph of being an American working woman, and the family's fight began. As they worked to get back on their feet, Betsy took matters into her own hands as well: she started babysitting at the age of twelve, and when she was old enough to work, she started waitressing. Forever would it be implanted in her mind: her mother in that tight black dress, the underdog and least expected who saved the day.

Betsy said she knew in that moment she was no longer a girl. She always pitched in the best she could: babysitting, making clothes, baking, anything to keep the wolves of abject poverty from the door. She had seen it ratcheting up the tensions of their household, seen the worry, the disappointment and the wretched hope against hope that somehow things would be different. For her, they actually would—she'd get an education, buy a home, earn a good income, even run for president—but throughout her career she'd still seek to understand it. She couldn't let what happened to her family go. Why was it that the people she loved—good people, decent people, hardworking people—seemed unable to rise above an unending cycle of poverty? What kind of society would pulverize its citizens with such persistent trauma? She would spend her life trying to answer those questions and develop solutions that might resolve those problems. And ultimately her quest would lead her straight into politics.

Years later, Betsy would become Senator Warren, and she would become a symbol of what happens when women lead, but there was another moment between Betsy and her mom, during the years she was a long-limbed teen in high school, that demonstrates the core of her being. The scene: She's in her bedroom, standing on her bed, raging, full-on mouthing off in a shouting match with her mom . . . about what? Her education. The big brawl wasn't about whether she could go to a party or about some bad boy she'd been caught hooking up with—all the things a mother-daughter rumpus usually entails at that age. They are both in prime position for the fight, arms folded, each at her breaking point. "She had been yelling at me," Warren writes in *This Fight Is Our Fight*. "Why was I so special that I had to go to college? Did I think I was better than everyone else in the family? Where would the money come from?"

But she *was* special, and Pauline knew it. In fact, unlike her mother, Betsy was the type who wanted to work when

SHE-RO
IN THE
MAKING

she grew up, and had decided on her career in second grade! She was a *badass* who'd skipped the sixth grade at Wilson Elementary School. Baby girl was smart, and her parents eventually realized the best way to empower their daughter's future was to offer her the best education they could afford. For them, that meant moving to Oklahoma City and buying a home in a better school district. There, Betsy attended Northwest Classen, where she graduated at sixteen years old. *Dang!*

While there, she joined the Cygnet Pep Club debate team.

On that high school debate team, she was the anchor, the linchpin, the closer, the ball-buster, the final nail in her opposition's coffin, helping her team bury their opponents in an avalanche of defeat. Her trademark, or *rep*, was identified by the deck of index cards she carried with her constantly and kept at the ready so she could whip out a fist of facts to annihilate the unwitting, uninformed who dared underestimate her as just some bony girl. She was a champion, a warrior. That was her problem, her mother insisted; smart girls were not the woman of any man's dreams.

In addition to being the keeper of that box of facts and notes, she was the school's tour guide, shepherding visitors through the halls. She was the school's morning greeter, the announcer who read messages over the school's PA system, which required a membership to the Announcers Club, by the way. She even achieved things to make her mother proud, like when she won the Betty Crocker Homemaker of Tomorrow

Award, and could "memorize the butterfat content of heavy cream and how to tie off a lazy daisy stitch." See, even when she was Betsy, a little lass, Elizabeth Warren has always been about taking care of business.

But in high school, all the cool categories that conferred street cred eluded Betsy. She seemed to be the only person she knew whose parents couldn't make ends meet. Her father always dropped her off a block from the schoolyard, just so the mean girls she was sure were lurking would not comment in their nasty, mouthy kind of way on their broken-down car. She knew that her life could be more than this, and the lessons of Mrs. Lee stayed crystal clear: more education would be her way out.

SHE APPLIED FOR scholarships, and as a skilled debater, the girl from small-town Norman, Oklahoma, earned scholarships to not one but two prestigious universities: George Washington and Northwestern University. She chose George Washington because it allowed her a full debate scholarship and federal loans. It wasn't about the parties or the sports teams—Betsy was focused on what would give her the best future. She keeps it 100 at all times. Yet still, she's everywoman, and has had to learn many lessons before embracing her crown like the rest of us. So the best way to describe this next chapter of her life is: It's Complicated.

★ ★ ★ ★ ★ ★ ★ ★ ★ ★ ★

WOMAN

If you don't have a seat at the table, you're probably on the menu.

—ELIZABETH WARREN

SCHOLAR SENSEI

Free your mind and the rest will follow.

—En Vogue, "Free Your Mind"

As expected, college felt like heaven to Betsy. Not only was she on track to become a teacher, but for the first time she experienced financial freedom. Her scholarships, student loans, and work-study job put her on equal footing with most of her classmates and actually offered a little extra financial support as well. After growing up in small-town Oklahoma, she was getting a cultural education too: at GWU she was meeting people of different ethnicities and students from different countries, and was going to the ballet or the theater in her spare time. Following her heart had brought Betsy to a world she never dreamed she'd be part of. But in her sophomore year, it was her mother's dream that came true.

"Will you marry me?" Jim Warren asked her. And she said yes, in a New York nanosecond.

Ugh.

Sis, it hadn't come out of nowhere; he had been her high school boyfriend (they met on the debate team, classic Liz) and was the only guy she had ever dated. He was a bit older than she was and had gotten a job at the computing giant IBM. Jim was a catch, and Betsy, still steeped in her mother's perception of the world, despite what Mrs. Lee had told her, tried to ride happily off into the sunset. Liz did what many young women have done when at the top of their game. She dropped it all for a man.

Ugh.

Her mother never thought Liz would be so lucky. By the time Jim asked her, it was a no-brainer that she should say yes. Suddenly, our heroine was thrown back into the 1950s Stepford-wife experience. She dropped out of college and put her ambitions aside to start a family with Jim. He was nice, there was nothing wrong with him personally. But in this new life she would need to cover up her inconvenient ambition with a virtuoso housewife's veneer. Liz would learn quickly that what makes sense for your mother does not always make sense for you.

THANKFULLY, OUR LIZ is not one to be held back. She may be responsible. She may be honest. But she is no pushover.

As is so often true for new wives and mothers, Liz struggled to reckon with herself, instead she reconciled her own form of freedom with the example her parents had set. She and Jim moved to a comfortable home in Houston, where finally she was easily a member of the middle class, but the gloves, the bridge clubs, the perfectly pinned hats, and the bows just-so, oh Lord help her, they never captured her inquisitive mind. Like many women who came before her, she needed a deeper existence than cooking, cleaning, and do-it-yourself carpet and tile. Luckily, her generation was beginning to break out of the past pressures of those who came before them. Within two years of entering homemaker-hood, our heroine was back in school. In 1970 she finished her BS at the University of Houston, and not long after, she and Jim moved to New Jersey for his job. There, she became a teacher, a speech pathologist, for children with special needs. Dream Number 1: *check!*

As a teacher, Liz loved her students and the value they brought to her life—as a teacher she had found her life calling, the way she had felt all those years ago back in Mrs. Lee's reading group. Then, surprise! She was pregnant, and with that, her job was on the line. She did her best to hide it—she wore baggy clothes, she puked quietly in the bathroom—and it worked for about six months. But, honey, there is only so much one can do to hide what would grow to look like a yoga ball in her belly.

According to the Board of Education's rules, she couldn't

work beyond a certain term while pregnant, so Liz was out of commission for the summer, and her spot was given to someone else for the following school year. (There has been controversy over whether she was fired or not . . . She was: The Board of Education renewed her contract but her boss fired her.) Thank goodness, years later, pregnancy discrimination would become a political issue, and by 1978 the Supreme Court would pass the Pregnancy Discrimination Act. Today women in the United States have the legal right to carry their big bellies to work as long as they want, and many states have maternity and paternity leave. For Warren, though, that progress didn't come soon enough.

But she wouldn't be kept down for long: two years later, Liz convinced Jim to let her go to law school. (Let her go? **side-eye**) She loved her family and the child she had with Jim, but she wanted—no, *needed*—more intellectual stimulation. With Amelia, now a toddler, in tow, she enrolled at Rutgers University. Many women decide to stay with their children full-time. It's good for some, and stay-at-home moms deserve praise, but the point is that it's a *choice*. And our sensei scholar was meant to learn and to teach just as much as she was meant to be a mother.

The mantra of most JD students sounds something like "This too shall pass . . ." Law school is hard. It's a fact. But, uh, in Liz's own words: "I took to law school like a pig takes to mud." She loved it.

Liz went straight for the tough stuff—finance and contract law. "I loved the idea of gaining mastery over money," she says in her book. She loved manipulating, managing, wrestling down the one thing that could have changed her parents' lives for the better—money. So while our career course in life often seems like a safe bet or a strategic decision, so often it is also an exploration of our own souls. And in this case for Liz, that decision began a decades-long journey, a journey that would define her entire career: to determine why families struggle, and to create clear solutions that will help them succeed as she had.

While she flipped through heavy textbooks of contract law in between packing lunchboxes, one would think her husband would be so impressed by her that he'd break into an electric slide dance and dab every time she entered a room. She did the same papers and completed the same exams as her colleagues, and she did it through every daily obstacle, sleepless nights, and some tears of exhaustion, of course. She even did some of it while pregnant, and with a toddler! (Eek, think of the hormones, ladies!!!) Her son, Alexander, came along after she graduated, and the growing family moved back to Texas.

She'd been teaching at night and at Sunday school, since no one would hire a mother of two.

But in Jim's mind, he had made concessions. He had made allowances for her, maybe one too many, because he never seemed to be able to get what he really wanted. He needed a wife, the traditional kind, to bring him his slippers and have his meals ready on time. Liz always seemed to be aloft in a daydream, letting dinner burn or leaving dishes in the sink while she was busy studying. She was trying, he could see that, but she just couldn't get it quite right. Liz herself seemed hemmed in by her own conflicting desires. Wasn't there some way for a woman to raise the children she loved, become absorbed in the thinking she loved, and satisfy her husband at the same time? Two years after her graduation and ten years after they married, Jim and Liz separated, amicably, both realizing they were in an untenable situation.

Elizabeth pierced the veil of the life her mother had warned her to avoid. Singledom. Spinsterhood. Others would call her a queen who knows her own heart.

Liz's time as a single parent would leave an imprint on her politics for decades to come. Issues that would help working moms, like creating stability for low-income workers, keeping Planned Parenthood funded, and making childcare affordable affected her and a generation of single and divorced mothers. Thankfully for Liz, while she was a single parent, her family members, like the magical Aunt Bee, helped her through the tough task of raising kids.

As Warren tells it decades later: "Childcare should be a fundamental right, period. I remember how hard it was to find affordable, high-quality childcare for my two kids when

I was a working mom—and it's a zillion times harder today. At the end of my rope, I called my seventy-eight-year-old Aunt Bee in Oklahoma and broke down, telling her between tears that I couldn't make it work and had to quit my job. Then Aunt Bee said eleven words that changed my life forever: 'I can't get there tomorrow, but I can come on Thursday.' Two days later, she arrived at the airport with seven suitcases and a Pekingese named Buddy—and stayed for sixteen years."

As a single mother, Elizabeth was belly-deep in the pit of what poverty can feel like for many women. Even today, nearly half of single parents in America live in poverty. For those of us who haven't lived it: imagine having a child, or even two or three, and having to pay for groceries, childcare, and ideally extracurricular activities so your little one can have a brighter future. Elizabeth Warren speaks to the lives of women and the future paths for girls so that things can be better going forward. She's the captain leading the army, and we're following.

THE FIRST GENTLEMAN

Whatta man, Whatta man
Whatta mighty good man.
—Salt-N-Pepa, "Whatta Man"

"I'll celebrate living in [an] America where everyone can marry their own Bruce," Elizabeth once said in an interview.

About a year after her divorce, Liz met Bruce Mann, a tall, scholarly man. It was exactly what you'd expect it to be—a love story with educational overtones. They were at a conference. It was a hot day in Key Biscayne, Florida, in more than one way. **wink** It was a conference full of professors, so Lord there was a lot of chatter. Mann was coming out of a workshop when he looked up and saw the ball of light and energy that is Elizabeth Warren standing across the large room.

She was talking to a group of people, and he instantly noticed her glow. Yassss, girl. He described her in a CNN interview as "lively" and "energetic" and he was wowed by her. He had to find out who she was. It was a delicious case of love at first sight, as the hopeless romantics would describe it. The meeting of his twin soul is how the woo-woo romantics describe it. He went over to talk to her . . . but then he just sort of stood there.

It took her longer to notice him back.

After all, it was Warren at a conference—she was focused on the topics at hand. She was also a single mother away from her two small kids; she was there to take care of business and then get back home.

The next day he walked into a workshop wearing shorts. Oh, honey. He had nice calves and the thighs of a runner, which is how Elizabeth describes how he finally caught her attention—strength. Hello, handsome. She began to engage.

Over the next few months, they started spending time together in a different way that was not conference-like at all. There was serious attraction—tons of heat, baby. Mann was a man who knew what he wanted. He invited her to one of his classes at the University of Connecticut to see him in action, and when she saw him moving around with such a deep command and passion for law, filling the minds of his students with his intellect, Liz sat back observing, just love jonesin' like crazy for that man.

She was hooked. In that moment, her life had changed suddenly again; she knew that he was the love of her life. After class, they walked around campus.

"How was it?" he asked.

"Will you marry me?" she answered, and she wasn't joking. He understood her well enough to know that she wasn't.

A few months later, they were indeed married. "Yes, she proposed. She's Warren—she saw what she wanted and she went for it!" he told CNN.

She had met a man who absolutely rocked her world. She discovered in so many ways that what her mother had been telling her was true, but not exactly right. Marriage wasn't about codependency but partnership, and Bruce Mann was just her kind of partner. They were so much alike, and so different. Bruce was also a university professor man, a quiet, deep-thinking man, and a lawyerly hunk. He was the anchor and she was the stormy sea. He wasn't stuck on gender roles and division of labor. He was confident in his own identity, so he didn't need her to be anything other than who she was. And that felt good, really good, to a woman who had so often felt out of place. "I don't want to be married to somebody like me, I want to be married to somebody like him," she says.

IT WAS 1980 when they were married; the start of a decade that would see the rise of graffiti, Atari, Rubik's Cubes, Salt-N-Pepa, Bruce Springsteen, the Sony Walkman, Members Only jackets, and a new dawn of *radical*. They hadn't known each other more than a year. For his love, Mann would fly from

Connecticut to Houston, where Liz and her children lived, every weekend. He volunteered on the kids' soccer teams and attended parent-teacher conferences with Liz. Amelia, seven, and Alex, three, called him Dad. Eventually he would make the decision to leave his job at UCONN completely to be with his family. No longer would Liz need to fit into the way of a world—she had created her own.

Decades later, the *smoking hot* heat of their partnership remains—they're often shown together in their snuggly sweaters taking long walks by Fresh Pond in Cambridge, where they go to relax. As empty nesters, they continue to work on their careers, and that's what keeps the romance alive—well that, and their afternoon dates at the Lincoln Memorial, because that's how smart people date. It's where he takes her to get a dose of inspiration when the congressional fights get tough on her. Because there are tough days for even a powerhouse like Elizabeth Warren. During elections, they cozy up with beer and popcorn and flip back and forth between trashy TV and the race, just like the rest of us.

Strong woman, warrior and all, Warren can't help but refer to her hubby as "my sweetie" this and "my sweetie" that, signifying the flirty, playful nature of this couple. He's a man who listens. He gives his lioness room to shine, and is fine either sitting in the back row or standing by her side, depending on what she needs. As she said in a 2015 Facebook post, "Throughout my career, and all the unexpected twists and turns, [Bruce] has never once discouraged me from taking on a fight. He's always believed that if I wanted people to listen to my ideas, I might as well shout from the highest mountain I could find."

He's supportive when she tells the world that she's going to run for president. He's that sturdy shoulder, whether at her swearing-in to the Senate or on the presidential campaign trail.

Every Queen of the Resistance deserves a king like Bruce in her corner, and Liz is quick to praise him for his valor. On their anniversary she also posted,

> *Last night when I got home, Bruce met me with a sweeping "ta-da!" and flung open the door to the hall closet. New shelf. Hooks. A place for grocery bags. "Happy Early Anniversary!" Ok, that may not seem very romantic, but I LOVE organized closets. (Yes, I hang all my jackets together, arranged by color.) But I have zero time to hang a shelf and even less time to get out the drill and put up some hooks. The new shelf and hooks (and Bruce's enthusiasm for them) made me laugh—and reminded me just how sweet and thoughtful Bruce always is. Back when I proposed to Bruce, I knew he was pretty special. But through decades of ups and downs—kids, dogs, moves, living in*

separate cities, deaths in the family, and on and on—he's turned out to be even more special than I originally thought. He even hangs a shelf on occasions like this. I'm a very lucky woman.

Bruce Mann is a leading man.

LOVE IS MY

COFFEE

I HAVE A PLAN FOR THAT

Are we gladiators or are we bitches?

—Olivia Pope, in *Scandal*

In 1981, a year after she had remarried, another love that equally matured and flowered in Liz's life was her career. She had always been driven, and the sort of woman who, when she put her mind to a task, would get it done. Liz will expand time, flex walls, and the Earth as we know it will reconfigure if need be. Internally she had grown since her days at George Washington; she no longer needed permission to be herself, a whole woman—dashing, daring, dynamic, determined.

Then there were her politics. . . .

Back when she was in her twenties, teaching business and finance classes at the University of Houston, Liz was a Republican.

Really, *shocking*!

Now Warren's "the North Star" of the left!

The "Warren Wing of the Democratic Party"!

Since 2014, progressives have been working on "Draft Warren" campaigns!

She's a progressive *icon*!

A lot of life-changing magic would happen in those years as Liz blossomed from Houston to Harvard, and into a progressive and finance superhero—like Billy Batson becoming Shazam!, it was a long process. Today, Sen. Elizabeth Warren doesn't talk much about her days in the Republican camp—*who would,* unless you're as cool as Michael Steele. You know, it's sort of like that hair phase you went through in the '80s, the one that you live to forget. *Don't you dare judge her!* Liz was certainly a registered Republican during the time she first lived in Pennsylvania and Massachusetts. Today it would be a walk of shame down memory lane for Liz, but let's be clear: she was not anti–gay rights or abortion and did not promote the conservative social agenda. She was focused on economic policy, period. In her mind, she could vote for any candidate. "I voted—sometimes voted for Democrats, sometimes voted for Republicans—but never thought of myself, never had to frame myself in political terms," she said in an interview with *Politico.* She also noted that in the six presidential elections she voted in before 1996, she only voted for one Republican, Gerald Ford. After that she was converted. So, come on, Liz wasn't a *real* Republican, right? She was.

As we've discussed, Liz did not grow up in a political home

or ensconced in that environment, and as she explained it, "I was just never very political." She *was* a professor, and one who was abducted into the ideology of Reaganomics, the economic policies of President Ronald Reagan that were focused on tax reductions and an unrestricted free market for businesses. Reaganomics had built a following known as the Law and Economics movement during the 1970s and 1980s while Liz was at the beginning of her legal career at Rutgers. The Law and Economics movement was founded by a law professor named Henry Manne and was funded by wealthy conservatives in order to, according to *Politico*, "inject some business-oriented thinking in the relatively liberal environs of elite American law schools." They would host these little conferences around the country for law professors and judges known as "summer camps" or "Manne Camps"—you know, the kind where they pin you in a strange hotel with free sandwiches and cocktail hours to make up for the day-long lectures. But before you judge her attendance there, think about Bikram yoga for a little perspective—you had no idea that your best workout's ideology had been compromised! It was at one of those conferences at the Manne's Law and Economics Center where she met Bruce. "As we've always said, something good came from Law and Economics, I found my sweetie," she said. "That should be a good country-western song, don't you think." LOL, no, lady.

Today Senator Warren advocates for fair trade. As a young

"I'VE GOT A PLAN FOR THAT."

lawyer, Liz believed that the free markets worked and that they should be left free to do what they wanted. Mainly she went along with the status quo, largely under the influence of her surroundings and the prevailing academic attitudes in the legal profession; she hadn't formed her own theories yet. At the time she deeply believed this ideology and it was entrenched in her overall identity so much so that it led her to conduct a major project.

It was in 1981 that things started to take a drastic turn, leaving our heroine's eyes opened. This is when Elizabeth Warren got *woke*!

Here's how her conversion went down, sis: She was an academic with a big appetite for research. She and her friends Jay Westbrook and Teresa Sullivan at Harvard Law School, let's call them the A-Team, decided to embark on a voyage to find answers about why so many Americans were filing for bankruptcy. Their mission was to see if the conventional wisdom about bankruptcy was true, namely whether there was a connection between bankruptcy and those who had proven themselves fiscally irresponsible—meaning they had signed up for car leases that they could not afford, were spending too much on duds at Alexander's Department Store (#throw back), and so on. Liz was the MacGyver, most skeptical, and eager to blast the bad guys.

She strongly believed that she knew what would be the conclusion of their research. At the time, Warren believed that Americans—the *good ones* who had been more frugal and responsible with their finances and who'd just reorganize their closets for stylish inspiration instead of going on shopping sprees they could not afford—needed to know that *other Americans* were playing unfair and putting the nation at risk. "My take on this, my thrust, what I was going to do, is I was going to expose these people who were taking advantage of the rest of us by hauling off to bankruptcy and just charging debts that they really could repay, or who'd been irresponsible in running up debts," she told *Politico.* Congress had just made changes to strengthen financial protections for families. But she also discovered that these new laws were based on a series of antiquated, unproven presumptions about the reasons for financial failure.

True to American puritanical roots, and a persistently skewed tendency to assign virtue to the rich and scurrilous blame to the poor, those presumptions went like this: the people who file for bankruptcy are the people who will always and forever be struggling on the edges of poverty. They are the lazy, the slovenly, the ultra-consumers who buy more than they can afford, waste loads of cash on clothes and televisions but don't take care of their basic needs. The government's explanation was that these people weren't willing to work as hard—that's why they were in those positions in the first place.

It was generally believed that people in bankruptcy have spent money recklessly on sneakers and other personal goods instead of saving more and spending less. The poor and bankrupt were the bottom-feeders, the miscreants, the unwashed, according to this portrait.

While she initially believed some version of this narrative, Warren ultimately led the charge to uncover the truth, and to amass more scientifically sound research about why people in our economy fail.

Meanwhile, the financial troubles of the 1980s began to affect her brothers' lives. One of her brothers, John, had worked in construction most of his life, and the oil shortages of the 1980s had wiped out most of his opportunity in Oklahoma. David worked in the oil business, delivering supplies to the oil rigs in different parts of the state. His income dried up as his customers' cash flow was affected by shortages. Long story short, his business fell apart.

Once again, Warren's own family narrative seemed to fly in the face of America's conventional financial wisdom. She had seen her father work hard against the odds to defend the security of his family. Her brothers had both served in the military, and they knew the value of discipline and restraint. So, what was the deal? What were the reasons that more and more families fell into debt and had to shut down and start over? Was the American dream something that could sustain Liz's children and future grandchildren as a viable goal? Or had it become a myth, a specter that they would reach for and perhaps never achieve?

She needed to know the truth.

Warren's A-team traversed the country and acquired thousands of bankruptcy reports from different states. In that data, they discovered quite a different story from what was being portrayed, sis. Ninety percent of the bankruptcies in the nation were due to job loss, medical problems, divorce, or death of a spouse—not laziness!

The research showed that when Americans experienced a life-changing event, they were very often knocked off course and blown apart financially. The discovery left Warren and her crew at a loss. How was the economy thriving if so many hardworking people were losing their jobs and filing for bankruptcy?

Liz had grown up in Oklahoma, a predominantly blue state at the time. She later speculated that her parents leaned toward New Deal Democrats. Once she knew the truth about what was happening in America, that's when she got *woke*!

One of her friends told *Politico,* "She really did have a 'Road to Damascus' conversion when she saw the bankrupt consumers really were suffering—forced into bankruptcy by illness, firing or divorce—and not predators."

Liz and her A-team published a book about their studies in 1989, *As We Forgive Our Debtors.*

She would not fully convert to the Democratic Party for years; though her ideology had changed she didn't make a partisan move until years later. But she was presented with new information and chose to follow the truth.

The economy was "thriving." Well, sure, but only if thriving meant only a small percentage of entities were sustaining and benefiting from the stock market. Everyone else was struggling to keep up. But if anyone knew about this, they weren't being vocal enough and getting through to the American people. Liz became that person.

FOR THE LOVE OF JUSTICE

For the love of money, people will rob their own brother.

—The O'Jays, "For the Love of Money"

Elizabeth's study of bankruptcy took her to the very heart of America, where capitalism and democracy meet. She learned the hard way that capitalism was only promoting the few in the economy, but that the situation could change with our system of representative democracy if we elevate the right people to run government.

"Capitalism" is treated like a dirty word, but it's not. Senator Warren has vowed that she's a capitalist. In fact, that's what she believes separates her from progressive Bernie Sanders. "He's a socialist; I believe in markets," she'd say. What's the deal with American capitalism, sis, and how does this issue relate to the life, times, and rise of Elizabeth Warren? Let's take a walk—or run a marathon—through our drama.

True democracy suggests that there is an "inalienable"

spark of the divine in every human being, and that each person has an inherent, sacred right to participate in the collective decisions that affect their future. Under our system, citizens acknowledge class difference and elect a group of representatives who make collective decisions on behalf of the people. America has constantly wrestled with the quest to determine who has the right to decide the future policies of the nation, the people or the powers that be.

When Elizabeth's parents were born, the legendary titans of industry were in their heyday—Cornelius Vanderbilt, the railroad builder; J. P. Morgan the financier; John D. Rockefeller of Standard Oil; and Andrew Carnegie, the steel magnate. These men amassed great personal wealth in the mid-to-late 1800s during the Industrial Revolution, when the nation had no personal income tax, no corporate taxes, and no inheritance taxes. There were also no fair labor laws, no workers' compensation, no mandatory lunch breaks, no vacation time, no health benefits, and no minimum wage.

People began to resent the cavorting of the super-rich while many citizens worked six days a week in twelve-hour shifts with little to no breaks. Often they faced working environments riddled with safety hazards, lethal toxins, sweltering heat, and unsanitary conditions. At the turn of the century, notions began to arise among the working class that suggested all people on Wall Street did was buy and trade paper! They did not contribute goods to the market like the workers whose labor fueled the manufacturing dominance of the United States for much of the twentieth century.

The bitter conflicts and politics that arose behind these sentiments led to the passage of the Sixteenth Amendment, ratified in 1913, not long after Elizabeth's parents were born. It gave Congress the right to assess and collect taxes as a way to recapture a portion of the wealth the people had created for public use—essentially, it established the income tax as we know it today.

That was also the beginning of the end of unimaginable wealth in America. After the implementation of personal income taxes along with all the other requirements demanded by labor, which became conventions of American business—retirement plans, employer-sponsored health insurance, eight-hour workdays, and five-day workweeks, for example—the ability to amass legendary fortunes in this country was greatly reduced. It may sound surprising, but to an extent, it really did work. For example, Jeff Bezos, the owner of Amazon, is considered the richest man in the United States today. His fortune of $108 billion is only one-third of what Andrew Carnegie owned at the height of his wealth, estimated at $385 billion in 2020 dollars, or John D. Rockefeller's fortune, estimated to be the equivalent of $318 billion at its height.

Each of those provisions demanded by fair labor practices required funding in the form of a range of new taxes on businesses and the wealthy. Government regulation required some of the benefits of labor to go to the masses of people who worked in these institutions. These more democratic ideas asserted that workers were the true "makers," instrumental to the corporations' success and the creation of individual wealth for the owners. The shareholders could keep a large chunk of the profits, but some of those profits should benefit the labor forces who created them. Some of these measures were implemented just before Elizabeth's parents were born and others were implemented throughout the first two-thirds of their lives. Still, tensions around who should get the lion's share of corporate profits remain a defining issue in politics and business.

After the stock market crash of 1929, populist pressures again demanded that government take a central role in digging the millions of unemployed American families out of the ditch they had found themselves in due to the "exuberance" of Wall Street.

Exuberance in this context refers to an environment where people are so giddy about the opportunity to make a profit through stock trades that they spend too little time doing the due diligence required to ensure their investment is sound. If fewer people are checking investments closely, less-scrupulous manipulators of the market can introduce stocks not based on anything of real value. If these kinds of investments permeate the market, the minute an investor demands real cash for her investment or learns what is really happening inside these trades, the market will crash. The more widely a flimsy stock has been traded, the more unwieldy the entire system becomes, like a house of cards that tumbles at the first puff of wind, once the insufficiency is discovered.

In 1929 this disaster infamously came to pass, and the stock market crash left millions of Americans destitute for many years. It left deep scars. As we learned from the life and times of Liz's parents, it was the government that dug the everyday Americans out of the ditch of the Great Depression.

WARREN'S VISION FOR America looks a lot like the New Deal programs that Franklin Roosevelt implemented to drive the nation's recovery. Those programs put millions of Americans to work through the Works Progress Administration (WPA), which paid Americans to rebuild highways and roads. They also built new schools, libraries, post offices, athletic stadiums, and hospitals; improved air landing fields and army camps; made books for the blind; and more. In six years, the WPA employed 8 million workers. The WPA Federal Theatre Project put thousands of creative writers, actors, playwrights, and musicians to work and entertained a total of 60 million people by the time it was over. The Civilian Conservation Corps put young men to work in pest control, land irrigation, planting trees, enriching soil, fire prevention, and other projects. In this way, the federal government put Americans back to work.

Tens of billions of dollars in federal resources, partially available due to the implementation of personal income tax and corporate taxes years earlier, were invested in jump-starting the American labor force, and it worked. In addition to the WPA efforts, powerful federal regulatory authorities were developed to monitor the transactions of Wall Street and to administer billions in federal resources. The programs that redistributed wealth include Social Security, Medicare, and Medicaid. On the financial-regulation side, the Securities and Exchange Commission (SEC) monitored corporate abuses and stock trades, the Federal Deposit Insurance Corporation (FDIC) backed every deposit in certified American banks up to a certain limit, and the Glass–Steagall Act regulated bank speculation as tools to limit Wall Street "exuberance" to viable financial vehicles.

This is the economy Elizabeth inherited when she was born in 1949. It could thank the regulatory power invested in the federal government for its relative stability. Affordable public housing programs helped protect against homelessness, and labor regulations mandated standards of workplace safety. Social Security took care of the elderly who had paid their dues and could no longer work, and Medicare and Medicaid, among other health programs, helped the most vulnerable to access healthcare.

As mentioned previously, education, another vital part of a strong middle class, also received federal funding.

Ultimately, during Elizabeth's lifetime, the federal government would grow to be the largest employer in the entire United States, and a force that would implement more democratic reforms than at any other time in American history. These changes altered American life and grew much of the American middle class as a force to be reckoned with, who expected the kind of social mobility to better neighborhoods, more elite schools, entrance to higher-paying jobs, and a way of life that Millennials would kill for today.

But it couldn't last forever. By the time Elizabeth Warren was investigating bankruptcy, President Ronald Reagan was in office and championing a rollback of the social programs and regulation that had helped the middle class more than those at the top. From the Reagan era on, America was dragged back to an environment where corporations dominated the landscape, without regard for the needs of the people.

These are the kinds of truths Elizabeth Warren began to discover as she explored the reasons behind the bankruptcy of the average American. She discovered that bankruptcy was nearly never due to some lazy couch potato who made sloppy financial decisions, those who were poor and likely always to be poor due to some inherent deficit (hmm, like being Black or an immigrant or a person of color?). Her findings belied that popular notion, a convenient misunderstanding among the wealthy that justified any lack of concern about the conditions their workers faced and absolved them of any obligation to do anything about it.

But that's where democracy comes in to create change! And contender Warren would enter the ring. Hurrah!

★ ★ ★ ★ ★ ★ ★ ★ ★ ★ ★

LEADER

I want to be pure. I want to be pristine.

—ELIZABETH WARREN, INTERVIEW WITH UNIVERSITY OF CALIFORNIA, BERKELEY, PROFESSOR HARRY KREISLER, MARCH 8, 2007

$UPERWOMAN

I'm not the kind of girl that you can let down
and think that everything's okay.
—Karyn White, "Superwoman"

A decade and a few universities later, Warren found her home teaching law at Harvard, where she had her women students *lit*. She became tenured after some time but it was her early years and her arrival at Harvard Law that left a mark on her time there. She was still a professor at the University of Texas School of Law when she invited Harvard professor Andrew Kaufman to a conference and they participated in a presentation together. In his words, he was "blown away by her"—he had never seen anyone rap law with such dynamism! Immediately he wrote a letter to Harvard's appointments committee suggesting that they invite her to teach there.

When she started, it was the fall of 1992, an unusual time at Harvard Law. There were only five women who had made tenure there, and the students were mad about it. Really mad. With their colored spandex, halter tops, and shoulder-padded black leather jackets, they occupied the hall in front of the dean's office to protest the lack of diversity on the faculty. It was *Judge Judy* gone Ivy League, honey, where lawsuits were filed by students. They were shouting about the need for more women of color on the faculty. It was a little *cray-cray*—which is sometimes fitting in acts of resistance. The students were put on trial for loitering. They had administrative hearings where hundreds of students came out in support of their peers, and the hearings lasted two days! It was a big ol' mess, honey, according to the bewildered ancient white male faculty who weren't used to this need for "diversity." And the students had a right to be angry. The number of women on the faculty in the early '90s had actually gone down. To five!

But the students had a plan or a theory.

In an interview with WBUR one of those students recalled some material that they'd created for the protest. The wording on the flyer stated the negative number in female faculty . . . but also there was a footnote . . . "This figure will improve to negative one if Elizabeth Warren accepts a position here."

(Okay but negative one?! What does that even mean, tho?!)

They were eagerly awaiting Warren's arrival. A large body of them held a vigil in support of her appointment outside of the building when she was offered the job.

And when she started, she did not disappoint. Her lectures were as masterly and polished as Olivia Pope's on *Scandal,* and the young women at Harvard were ready to be Professor Warren's gladiators and take charge of the broken system. Her classes had the intensity of an Orangetheory Fitness class, and her students would burst out of her ten A.M. lecture sweating, energized, and full of academia endorphins. The Warren would shoot out question after question after question and students would hustle to catch them like flying Frisbees. She was sharp and a little scary in a good way, intense, but also warm and fuzzy. It was Mrs. Lee's early influence, and all of those years teaching Sunday school; she was intellectual candy. She'd pull on those rimless glasses and it'd be a master class in law. She was the Oprah of law school—*you get an exam, you get an exam, you get an exam!* They loved her! And you could talk to Professor Warren, you know; she wasn't one of those snotty-nose, uppity types. She'd ask how your day was going. There was nothing to be afraid of; she'd patiently wait for your response. She'd go to your debate performance if you asked her. Professor W could break down law, contracts, and economic theories quicker than you could eat a Klondike bar, and these kids, especially the women, looked to her for more than legal expertise. She was an example. The Tao of Liz. *A woman* who had written books and *a woman* who was one of the most sought-after minds in her field. But even when the students looked to Professor W for some guidance on women's rights or how to navigate the patriarchal challenges that they had inherited since girlhood, the feminine mystique, or the fist of sexism they felt locked into right there on campus, she would steer the conversation ahead of the curve, toward areas that hadn't yet headlined in women's rights discussions. In her lane as a professor, Warren asked questions that pertained to women about money and policy. In order to experience real change, any underdog would have to break the spiderwebs of policy that have set women back for decades, especially women of color. *Money, money, money* was an important refrain that needed to be associated with social justice.

When Harvard offered her tenure, she was also teaching at the University of Pennsylvania and her students loved that their unusual law professor had actually gone into courtrooms and talked to real people about law and money. Ha-ha, what professor would think to do such a thing? Warren. She had drilled down into the research she was unearthing and challenged them to do the same, to get to the bottom of an issue.

In fact that's around the time she first met Barack Obama. He was just a young, ambitious guy who was having a party in Cambridge, Massachusetts, as a fundraiser for his run for US Senate in Illinois. Here's how Warren told it in 2011 at the University of Arkansas:

> *He holds his hand out. This is just like in the movies. And as I hold my hand out and as our fingers touch, he says to*

me: "Predatory lending." And then he just goes [on and on]. And I never get a word in. I never get a word in! And I'm just standing there. My hand's still in his hand and he's talking. And finally, he gets all the way to the end, and he gets this big grin. And he says: "Well?" And I say: "You had me at predatory lending."

Her work on American economics had become more important than ever.

Some of her students would assist her in that work. When she first started collecting information on bankruptcy in the early 1980s, when protective laws were mainly still in place, a quarter of a million people annually were filing for bankruptcy. By 1995 more than 1 million families a year were bankrupt.

Elizabeth knew these bankrupt families well: They were like her friends and neighbors in Oklahoma City. They were elderly couples who were wobbly on their feet, single mothers balancing babies on their laps. They were people she recognized, ordinary people who could have been her, had she not had the uncommon pluck to fight against prevailing traditions as a woman, become educated, and even risk raising her children alone—albeit with other family help—where she'd be judged, and use her law degree to put herself and her entire family on stable financial footing.

Her research revealed that the people declaring bankruptcy

OBAMA

were just like her parents, like her brothers, like the people she saw every day. They were everyday middle-class people. Again, there were three major reasons they were forced to file: losing their jobs, experiencing a major illness, and losing a spouse's income due to divorce or death. Usually they tried to bide a bit of time until they could figure a way out of debt, by using credit cards or taking out second mortgages to stem their financial bleeding. But these mechanisms only compounded the problem, leading them to a place where there was no hope of ever catching up.

As her study continued and the number of annual bankruptcies began to double, Warren noted that big businesses that failed were often given multiple opportunities to restructure their debt so they could continue operating. So she wondered, couldn't middle-class families be given similar opportunities? Seven hundred thousand people were filing for bankruptcy annually. This she discovered was due to a major deregulatory factor that changed the protections put in place after the Great Depression to limit the amount of interest a bank could charge on a loan. Loans are a form of bank speculation, and if banks lend money to a large number of individuals who are unable to repay those loans, then a bank is disbursing more money than it is taking on. Any smarty-pants knows that will eventually lead to disaster!

In the early 1990s, a Supreme Court decision had exempted

banks from having to abide by anti-usury rates and essentially gave the green light to banks to add fees and penalties to credit cards and charge interest rates as high as the market would bear. Elizabeth and her crew discovered that banks began to target people who were financially unstable. The less stable they were financially, the more likely they were to depend on credit as a means to stay above water. They were the ones who would have to pay the late fees and the steadily climbing interest rates. *Shoot,* they were the ones who were making the banks the most money.

Elizabeth decided not to sit back and be quiet about this. She started banging down the doors of public officials, **gutteral scream,** spitting fire, wanting to let lawmakers know what she and her researchers had discovered.

The Republicans and Democrats obviously had different views on the issue—like two siblings fighting over who should have the last cookie. Republicans were okay with individuals wading through the weeds on their own. Democrats wanted to fight for a solution, but without control of the House, they didn't have the political clout to pass legislation. Without that power, any progress was dead in the water.

Then there was Elizabeth Warren and her crew, the Harvard scholars, the A-team **cue sountrack.** They were not invested politically yet, but they had deeply studied the research in front of them. The data showed it all. Warren was invested in the facts, and what she discovered illustrated a big humanitarian issue. Simply put, Americans were being tricked, bamboozled, and the government needed to do something about it!

It was an acceptable ask of the government, given our history.

Warren was involved in two successful attempts to push back on the banking industry's plan to change bankruptcy law. In 1995 President Bill Clinton developed a nonpartisan blue-ribbon commission to study whether bankruptcy law should be changed. The commission would not be White House–led. It was to be an in-depth examination by appointed experts to reveal the facts surrounding the proposals for change. It would help the president bolster his mandates or appeals to Congress, if there was a proven case for reform. Warren was tapped for the nine-member bipartisan commission by a former Oklahoma congressman (and her former high school debate opponent) Rep. Mike Synar. Warren told *Politico,* "We hadn't seen each other in the intervening decades, but 14-year-old boys seem to remember 15-year-old girls who once beat them in [debate] tournament play."

The National Bankruptcy Review Commission, as it was called, needed a soldier they could trust. Someone not involved in politics, but someone invested in the data, the numbers, the facts of life, and that was Liz.

Hell no, she protested when Synar, the commission's chairman, approached her about the job of chief policy adviser.

He liked her passion for the truth. She said no, that she didn't want to get "muddy" in politics. The way she saw it, politics just wasn't her lane at that time. "Come and do this," he begged, "so we have good ideas to work with, and I promise, I will insulate you." He promised her protection, a common promise in the art of courtship, which in politics, especially for a nonpolitician, was vital. He was telling her she could just positively nerd out and provide the answers for the nation's families who needed her as they jogged along on a treadmill of debt. She'd be the brains, the boss, behind the scenes. Synar asked her for three good ideas. That's it, he promised, and he'd get them done.

Liz is a woman driven by principle. She didn't desire to be front and center. It was for the good of the cause that Liz decided to do it, sis. She began attending hearings and commuting between Boston and Washington. As she expected, the politics were repulsive. Bankrupt families were being bullied. The banks were *paying* "experts" to attend the hearings. As if that weren't appalling enough, she saw how ingrained the "politicking" was in the policy. The banks were asking for higher standards for those who qualified for bankruptcy. Therefore poor people who needed to declare bankruptcy wouldn't be able to use it until they had "achieved" a higher level of debt. Many of the bankers were financially paving the way for politicians and writing checks for their campaigns. The bankrupt people, of course, didn't have the resources to hire lawyers and defend themselves. Liz was there in the courtrooms, exposed to the political *ickiness* like never before.

Then after only a short time, just months into their hustle, Synar passed away due to brain cancer. Oh no. Who would sell the good ideas to Congress? "Sell them into fruition," as Mike had told her. She had other suitors on the commission who wanted to pick up the mantle and replace Synar in shepherding and caring for her research. But Liz turned them away. "I realized that either I step up or nobody does."

She knew that there was only one person she could fully trust with her data and research: herself. She would be the only person to make sure it translated properly to correct policies that struggling people needed corrected, and not just the men in the suits fighting about them. She would not let a politician take it over and twist her words to get what he wanted. No way, José.

Salty partisan advocates who were touting the same ideology as the banks had also been appointed to the commission; the banking lobby clearly had ears in the commission meetings. They realized the commission report would not likely side with them, so before the report was finished and voted on, the banking lobby began prowling Capitol Hill like wolves to begin framing the debate before the commission report could make an impact. The banking lobby crafted its own bill and began to try to find legislators to sponsor it.

So Warren did a bit of lobbying of her own. She and her

partners went on the offensive, meeting with labor interests, nonprofit consumer groups, and other advocates in a counterlobbying effort to inform members of Congress and their staff about the detriments of the bill. They were seriously outgunned by the banking lobby, who'd hired high-priced, well-connected lobbyists, some of whom were powerful former legislators. Finally, one day, Warren had the opportunity to sit down with the senator from Massachusetts, Ted Kennedy, a man who had influence on both sides of the aisle. If she could convince him, he would be a powerful ally to help defeat the banking legislation.

They talked for a long time. Warren's ability to articulate the depth of her research, her experiences in bankruptcy court, her personal interaction with victims of bankruptcy, and her years of experience as a professor and a lawyer allowed her to answer all the questions Senator Kennedy had about the bill. In the end, he became the linchpin in an effort that would ultimately stop the passage of that detrimental bill. Warren helped win another victory for democratic interests against the moneyed elite, but it would not last forever.

Ten years later, in 2005, the banking interests got what they had been working so hard for: a bill that made it harder for Americans to file for the kind of bankruptcy that would wipe out all their debts and help them start over with a clean slate. They were trying to figure out how to profit even more from people who were on the brink of financial collapse. Incredibly high interest rates that made credit-card debt almost impossible to pay off, the ability to raise interest rates for almost *any* reason, penalties and fees that pushed late payers and struggling card users further into debt were not enough.

Liz decided to launch an updated study of financial failure and found that the situation had not gotten better at all! To Liz, it was an urgent matter, and Congress was either not moving fast enough or, worse, was moving in the wrong direction. She published her book *The Two-Income Trap: Why Middle-Class Parents Are Going Broke* with her daughter, Amelia Warren, to educate families on the pitfalls in America's financial structure. In the research, she once again found that the issue wasn't that families were just a bunch of lazy goof-offs but that we had a *big* problem that had been overlooked—wages hadn't changed since the 1970s, while the cost of living had skyrocketed, doubled, tripled, and did a salsa doozy on American families, keeping them trapped in poverty and on the cliff of bankruptcy.

"I'm down there talking to them about it!" Warren said years later in a speech, her voice rising and her eyes widening. "I'm telling people and nobody wants to—*La, la, la. I can't hear you.* I fly down to Washington. I got to where I just made cold calls. I'd go see congressmen . . . I would explain what was happening, and how obviously they're packaging these things and selling them up the line [to the people]. They are selling grenades with the pins already removed. And they're going to explode!"

And then—BOOM! A few years later? The economy would explode.

SOUND THE ALARM!

Freedom and blood
I make my mark and fight for tomorrow.
—Tegan and Sara, "Proud"

It's 2008 and the economy is crashing. The eagle had landed. While financial institutions were saved from collapse by the government, so many other things fell apart. The stock market caved, and the housing market plummeted so bad that there were mass foreclosures, evictions, and unemployment. (Will give you the *tea* on that later.) Our heroine saw this coming, and she finally had the juice she needed to step in and really make changes.

She was appointed to *lead* the Congressional Oversight Panel responsible for overseeing the $700 billion Troubled Asset Relief Program (TARP) that would save the financial system. **clapping, clapping**

Her goals were "transparency, accountability, and clarity—an articulation of what the government policies are and explanation of what's going on," she said in a tender moment with Jon Stewart on *The Daily Show,* a scene that solidified her as a trusted voice in the matter. The American people had always been taught to think the country was too big to fail. Families were learning that they'd lost their businesses or their jobs—that at the opposite end of the American dream was bankruptcy. How could this happen? Sis, Warren knew how to explain why. Stewart said that her discussion on his show was one of the clearest explanations he had heard. The problem with politics is that it often feels too far removed from Mom and Pop's reality . . . until it's too close.

BUT LET'S BACK up for a minute. In the early 2000s, Liz decided to launch that updated study of financial failure of American families. By this time, the statistics were staggering and the single most powerful determinant of whether a family would go bankrupt was the presence of a child. This predictor was the same regardless of education or income, and the phenomenon was even affecting families with two working parents. So Warren decided to sound the alarm again.

Political pundits, many of whom are wealthy and therefore unaffected by these challenges, presumed the worst of the average American as usual. Once again, they incorrectly blamed conspicuous consumption for the rise in bankruptcy; all those outrageously priced sneakers and flat screen TVs—*that* was the reason families were failing financially. **sigh**

Warren and her daughter began to do the research for their book, and once again she discovered something different. Yes, families spent more on computers and communications than they had decades ago, but they also spent *less* on food and clothing. These families were not buying McMansions or fancy cars; they were living modestly very much like their parents had a generation before. But the cost of living had gone up precipitously—on food, clothing, housing, energy, transportation, gas, communications, college, *everything*! All of this while American workers were still making relatively the same wages they were making in the 1970s.

Meanwhile, corporations under the Bush administration had undertaken a massive effort to deregulate as much as they could. They broke the backs of the unions by refusing to move toward any union demands. Many companies like Walmart created innovations that consumers loved, but they did it on the backs of a non-unionized workforce who complained of inhumane corporate policies of no benefits, long hours, low wages, and few to no breaks that hearkened back to the economic model of the so-called Gilded Age.

BRING DOWN THE HOUSE

You should see me in a crown
I'm gonna run this nothing town.
—Billie Eilish, "You Should See Me in a Crown"

Liz's research uncovered some brutal truths. In just ten years, 15 million Americans had filed for bankruptcy, and as mentioned, sis, one of the key drivers was the cost of housing. Ever since the Great Depression, mortgage finance had been a foundation of the American economy. Before the expansion of international and business markets, a great deal of banking income came from the origination and servicing of mortgages.

For decades after the Great Depression, the cost of buying a home was relatively stable, but in 1997, the prices of homes started to rise. Yes, sister, yes. One reason was that very low interest rates, set by the Federal Reserve to help jump-start economic activity, encouraged speculators and developers to borrow money to buy land.

Aside from this, while the banks had been lobbying for

significant changes to bankruptcy laws, and Elizabeth Warren's attention was turned to that area of deregulation, the banks were also seeking to change the way they could trade mortgage-backed securities.

Mortgage-backed securities are a financial instrument created in the 1960s that allowed banks to bundle mortgages and sell them to a secondary market. Two organizations created by the federal government, Fannie Mae and Freddie Mac, bought and held mortgage-backed securities in the secondary market, and these securities were not only backed by land and houses; they were also insured by the federal government, if a mortgage failed. These two institutions also had means to service mortgages until the end of the loan period.

Because housing is considered one of the most important areas of finance in any nation, due to its impact on millions of families who own homes, regulations limited the way that banks could trade mortgage-backed securities. But banks wanted to be able to sell these securities on the stock market, to buy and trade mortgages in the same way any other stocks or securities were traded.

Noooooooooooo.

Noooooooooooo.

In 1999 the banks' lobbying paid off. They got their wish, and that's where the housing crisis really began.

As the price of land became cheaper, housing development began to boom. They were selling homes in a flash.

Many banks began to work with appraisers to determine the value of a home before they made a mortgage. In this unregulated market, appraisers were often prevailed upon by the banks to inflate the value of homes so the banks could make more money. This happened so frequently that it began to drive up the overall price of homes in the entire nation.

It became difficult for first-time homebuyers to get in the market, and sis, lenders began to target primarily African American, Latino, and senior homeowners who already owned homes to convince them to buy new ones, *grrr.* Often these buyers were placed into what lenders called the subprime market, meaning that the loans were more risky. Lenders were talking buyers out of mortgages they could afford and steering them toward mortgages with complex terms that they were more likely to default on.

For the mortgage broker, default was the government's problem. Banks make most of their money on the earliest payments of a mortgage, because most of those first payments go toward paying interest and very little toward the principal borrowed. So their preference was to make the loans, regardless of risk, bundle them, and sell them like hotcakes as mortgage securities, passing off the risk of default to someone else.

The problem occurred—well, you may be able to see a few problems already—when these securities were bundled, rebundled, and sold again. Brokers were determined to hide the riskier mortgages within a large bundle called triple-A. Some banks even began to sell bundles of mortgages they knew would fail, and then bet on the likelihood that those instruments would fail as yet another means to make money; those deals were called credit default swaps. These bad mortgages were sold all throughout the financial system—pension funds bought them, city governments bought them. The entire American financial system was polluted by these junk mortgages.

It all came crashing down when one by one the rate of default on these mortgages began to rise. Tens of thousands of homeowners discovered they were "underwater," meaning they had more of a loan on their homes than the houses were worth. This also meant that the banks left holding the actual mortgages were way overextended, to the point that many of them had to shut their doors. Fannie Mae and Freddie Mac, formerly success stories, were now themselves on the verge of bankruptcy.

Then the banking industry began to seize up. It stopped extending credit to businesses, both small and large. Wall Street giants couldn't handle it: Bear Stearns went under completely and Merrill Lynch almost went bankrupt.

In a strictly free market system, these kinds of market adjustments would take care of themselves; those companies that had made risky investments would simply close their doors or be purchased at a discount by other companies.

But some of the top financial companies on Wall Street were deeply involved in these shenanigans. Had they been allowed to fail, it could have brought down or significantly altered the entire system of international banking, not to mention done catastrophic damage to American markets. Thus these companies were deemed "too big to fail," meaning their failure would have such disastrous consequences to the financial positions of the entire country that the government would deem it in the best interests of the nation to step in and save them. And it did.

It also did not hurt that outgoing President George W. Bush had appointed Henry Paulson Jr., a former CEO and president of Goldman Sachs, to oversee the Treasury Department, which some critics felt was a bit like the fox guarding the henhouse. In the final six months that Bush was in the White House, Paulson advised the president and Congress that the banking industry was in serious trouble, and they believed him. They swiftly created the United States Economic Stabilization Fund, with Paulson at the helm. He would oversee the disbursement of $700 billion taken directly from the US Treasury to stabilize the financial system.

The toxic mortgages that had destabilized the banking system were called "troubled assets." So ultimately the Troubled Asset Relief Program, also run by Paulson, would be responsible for rescuing Wall Street banks by allowing the banks to start lending again.

Okay, but where's Waldo? Who's missing in all this bank chitter-chatter?

We, the people!

Millions of unwitting American homeowners were left drowning in debt!

Consumers were to blame for believing the promises of mortgage brokers. It wasn't the brokers' responsibility to be fully informative or even honest, was it?

JUST AS THE bank bailout was beginning to coalesce, Elizabeth Warren was called by the Senate Majority Leader, Harry Reid, to join a five-person Congressional Oversight Panel (COP) to monitor how Paulson and the Treasury Department managed the bailout. Sis, in the first seven weeks (!) after the TARP law had been passed, $172 billion had already been disbursed! All this and the COP monitoring panel hadn't yet had its first meeting in Washington. *By golly,* Liz thought.

She also learned that the oversight panel had very strict limitations. All the members of the panel had to keep their regular jobs. They could not engage in oversight full-time. Their only power was to hold hearings to inquire about issues related to the troubled asset program, but they had no ability to compel people to testify through subpoenas.

Are. You. Serious?

Liz was floored by the sheer volume of resources being thrown at banking executives who had been the source of the problem to begin with!

Billions of taxpayer dollars were being given away to for-profit businesses that skirted federal taxes, had no obligation to contribute to the well-being of the taxpayers who funded the bailout, and, since many were multinational corporations, no real fealty to the United States. All this while our national infrastructure was crumbling, while unemployment was on the rise, while the price of a college education was mainly out of reach for most American families. "We could have fixed our roads and bridges and public transportation. We could have launched universal preschool and made state universities affordable again. We could have doubled our federal investments in medical research and scientific research for the next twenty years," Warren says in her biography.

Usually, when the government loans money, it applies significant terms and requirements detailed in twenty or more pages of legal documents. In this instance, she discovered, some of the agreements were as few as two pages long (!), offering the banks an almost no-strings-attached multibillion-dollar loan.

Come *on*, what happened?!

Plus, the outgoing Bush administration had saddled the oversight committee with onerous reporting requirements, probably hoping that they would be so busy writing reports, they wouldn't have much of an opportunity to engage in any real oversight.

For Elizabeth Warren, that simply would not do. Limitations can't keep a queen down when the cause of democracy is at stake.

She was elected chair of the oversight committee in its first meeting, and since the committee would need to submit its first report in two weeks, she came up with a brilliant strategy to satisfy the requirement. Instead of producing a voluminous technical government report that would likely elicit a Washington yawn and be filed among millions of other government documents somewhere, they produced a brief, bold twenty-nine-page report that posed a series of questions to the Treasury Department.

First the report quantified the damage, something it seemed the government was trying to scuttle, in stark detail:

> *The headlines may belong to the financial markets and mega-institutions, but the recession has visited every household in the country. The crisis affects Americans' ability to pay their bills, to secure their retirement, to continue their educations, and to provide for their families. The unemployment rate is the highest it has been in fourteen years. In the last three months, 1.2 million Americans lost their jobs; 533,000 in November 2008 alone. Service sector*

employment levels, in particular, fell far faster than expected last month. One in ten mortgage holders is now in default, unable to make payments on their homes. More than 200,000 families and small businesses filed for bankruptcy protection in the last two months. Middle- and lower-income families have watched nervously as reductions in state funding threaten college access and credit card defaults are rising, and savings rates hover at zero. Shrinking retirement funds have left millions of retired people to wonder how they will pay basic expenses and millions more to wonder if they must continue working until they die.

These were breathtaking impacts. Often government reports are written by technical experts who are unused to communicating in colloquial terms, and sometimes they are purposely written to be so complicated that most people cannot understand them. This report was refreshing, inventive, and direct. A message broadcast to the people directly from the Government Printing Office.

And the COP report didn't stop there. It continues, after stating the facts, with a pattern of questioning that would set the tone for its work under Elizabeth Warren's leadership. Since writing a report in two weeks about a massive undertaking by the federal government was an untenable task, Warren decided to use the reporting requirement as a means of oversight and as a public opportunity to put the Treasury Department on notice:

> *What Is the Treasury Department's Strategy?*
>
> *What Have Financial Institutions Done with the Taxpayers' Money So Far?*
>
> *What Is Treasury Doing to Help the American Family?*

Then within each question she asked another series of questions:

> *What does Treasury think the specific causes of the financial crisis were, and how does its overall strategy address those causes?*
>
> *What specific metrics can Treasury cite to show the effects of the $250 billion spent so far . . . ?*
>
> *What steps has Treasury taken to reduce foreclosure, and have they been effective . . . ?*

The questions went on and on and on, sharp, pointed, and central to the problems at hand. Warren led the panel to create readable, engaging government documentation that asked the questions any taxpayer might have about the use of their resources. She used the limited authority of the panel for maximum gain to speak directly to the people, to Congress, and to the press, and it set the tone for COP's oversight of Treasury's actions.

Then she created a video and put it up on YouTube (!!!) so any American seeking information about the panel's work could check it out. *Yaassss!*

Then she had the panel set up a website so that anyone who wanted to could read it.

And, ladies, that's how you *boss*. **snap. snap.**

The panel's actions opened a floodgate of public commentary. People started writing in to the website, desperate for guidance. Warren had opened a portal to the anguish of the American people, something those in leadership roles are often afraid to do.

She was an advocate for democracy within a system that had been gobbled up by greedy entities who were happy to devour the entire system whole, and ignore the true meaning of democracy. For any moneymongers who believed they were the best stewards of public resources, the purveyors of the public good, and more capable of managing massive resources, Elizabeth begged to differ. And though she might have been the only one willing to stand up to a Goliath, she would start swinging and take her chances. The future of the country was at stake, and it needed an advocate, at least one person, fighting to save it.

Treasury responded to the report with a thirteen-page letter, which Warren's panel found mainly insufficient. COP launched their own independent investigations and fact-finding efforts, but they continued to demand answers of the Treasury Department.

Warren wanted these lenders to understand they were not above the law. So often they had stacked the deck themselves, hiring government executives who worked for regulatory bodies like the Security and Exchange Commission to come and work in their firms or placing firm faithfuls inside government agencies to be their eyes and ears and head off any criticism.

But she was an outsider, not a cozy member of a system that believed itself more important than the people it served. Sis, Liz wouldn't be caught dead in that company.

Her parents had been the victims of economic failure, and she grew up with hundreds of people in Oklahoma City who were buffeted by bank failure, crop failures. Their hopes and dreams had been dashed against the rocks and no one seemed to care how they suffered. Well, she would make certain they did not suffer in vain. She would be one Harvard professor, one Capitol Hill panelist, and ultimately one senator who would never forget where she came from.

★ ★ ★ ★ ★ ★ ★ ★ ★ ★ ★

RESISTANCE

Give me a chance,
I'll go to the
White House,
and I'll fight for
your family.

—ELIZABETH WARREN, FEBRUARY 19, 2020,
PRESIDENTIAL DEBATE, LAS VEGAS, NV

THE WARREN

It's time for me to take it
I'm the boss right now.
—Demi Lovato, "Confident"

Warren had gone a long way in defending the needs of the American people through her work in bankruptcy and her time overseeing TARP. But she knew the people needed something bigger, something more permanent, some kind of watchdog that could protect them far into the future. While she was still teaching at Harvard and chairing the oversight panel on TARP, she started to think about a more enduring way to help level the playing field between big corporate interests and everyday people.

At a meeting of advocacy groups hosted by the AFL-CIO, Warren floated an important new idea. What about creating a new agency of the federal government that oversaw all consumer lending—credit cards, mortgages, student loans, payday lending, car loans, any area of consumer finance that was required for daily life. She pointed out that there were laws on the books regulating consumer finance, but there were seven different agencies involved in monitoring banking's relationship with citizens, and no coordinated response by government to match the orchestrated activity of banks and lending institutions. In fact, banks often hired people who had previously served inside of these government agencies. It was like there was a revolving door between Wall Street and these federal offices that undermined the oversight effort overall. Warren felt all of that could be significantly altered by making one agency, a new agency, responsible for monitoring all of the consumer lending in the country.

round of applause

The groups she met with bought in, but they knew it would be an uphill battle. This was in 2009, nearly three decades since the Republicans had begun a successful onslaught against government oversight. President Ronald Reagan had made the battle against "big government" his rallying cry, and Republicans leaned into it to create a wedge between the people and the only entity with the power to put big business in check.

Some multinational corporations had incomes larger than many small nations, their own militarized security forces, and a cadre of politicians in every country to do their bidding, not that of the people who elected them. They had broken the back of labor unity and used bankruptcy and elegant accounting to get out from under the mandates of retirement pensions and health insurance premiums.

They had engineered a series of tax breaks for the rich beginning in the Reagan years. Back in the early 1980s, people would count the number of millionaires made in a year. These days, we can do that with billionaires.

Somehow, the wealthy had gotten the everyday man and woman to champion their cause. In fact, by taking up the charge against government, they were defeating the only force that had the power to impose the responsibilities of democracy. Warren knew all this: in attempting to establish a unified agency for consumer protection, she was fighting an uphill battle against corporate giants who would try to block her at every turn. She threw her hat in with the American people anyway and began a campaign to try to make this thing happen.

She had made some powerful allies in the Senate, including Ted Kennedy; Majority Whip Dick Durbin; Chuck Schumer, chair of the Senate Rules Committee; and Chris Dodd, chair of the Banking, Housing, and Urban Affairs Committee.

She also had friends in the House, including Brad Miller, who sat on the Financial Services Committee, but there was one more important voice she had to engage to get the support she would need: the chairman of Miller's committee, Barney Frank. He was brash, bold, demanding, and razor sharp. He was as conversant with the mystifying language of Wall Street as any banker. He did not suffer fools lightly, so if Warren was to meet with him she would need to be substantive and on point. Frank was skeptical about the possibilities of passing legislation that expanded the federal government after the hatchet job that had characterized the march of the last three decades.

People were infuriated about the excesses of Wall Street and the unprecedented "reward" they seemed to be getting for their misbehavior—$700 billion indeed, when millions of Americans were in debt up to their ears. The House and Senate banking committees were already working on a package of reforms; it was not only a regulatory imperative but a moral one. Action was required to restore people's trust in the banking system. But Frank wasn't sure that adding a new federal agency to the mix was wise. It might saddle the bill with too much baggage, which might derail any attempt to regulate at all.

Warren believed that this significant failure on Wall Street offered a chance to do something big. Sis, where Frank saw limitations, Liz saw opportunity. She was convincing, and Frank included her new agency in his Dodd–Frank Wall Street Reform and Consumer Protection Act. It was signed into law by President Barack Obama in 2010.

She created the Consumer Financial Protection Bureau. The CFPB has the power to sue companies and people who

WE CANNOT RUN A DEMOCRACY...
WITHOUT A STRONG
MIDDLE CLASS.
+76.33 3.54%
-1.33 4.19%
+67.12 1.35%
+23.90 4.25%
+33.21 5.22%
-3.12 5.42%
WALL ST
NEW YORK STOCK EXCHANGE

violate federal consumer laws. It is used to protect and educate consumers about financial products and services, especially those that are abusive. It also supervises banks and other financial institutions. A new chief is appointed by the president every five years. Obama named Warren assistant to the president and special advisor to the secretary of Treasury on the CFPB. Republicans were in a snit about her appointment due to what they associated with overly liberal views, but many consumer advocates and liberals were excited about her being the first director. And Obama had to rethink making his remarks official because the appointment would involve getting Senate approval, so instead he selected Ohio attorney general Richard Cordray as a recess appointment. It was a surprising twist of events, and disappointing to many, but Warren had still succeeded in her efforts. And she did what she said she would.

From all of us to you, thank you, Elizabeth Warren!

Neither Warren nor Obama viewed this as a loss. He told her to run for the Senate herself. A loss became a win.

LADY SENATOR

If I was you, I'd wanna be me too.

—Meghan Trainor, "Me Too"

Remember when you first stepped onto an ice-skating rink with those blades under your heels, and it felt like you'd never get your grip? You're holding on to the side rails *shook* as hell, and you're not skating, you're almost tiptoeing around the rink afraid that if you fall you'll cause a scene like *Nightmare on Elm Street* where you'll slit your face or someone else's in the escalator's motor chain? You're basically moving around the rink like you're in a scene from *Crawl*. Remember how you thought you'd never learn, and wanted to go home, it was frigid outside and your little fingers were icicles, and you had only come because your best homegirl begged you and there'd be spiked hot chocolate, but then you start moving and sliding and, girl, suddenly you're striding and gliding down the rink like a dang pro!

Well, Elizabeth Warren never thought in a million years she'd be in a position to run for elected office. Never. Until Republicans started messing with her and hindering her moves.

Now here she was in a statewide race against a popular Republican guy arguably better known for being good-looking than anything else: Scott Brown, who had cut into the Democratic dominance forged by Ted Kennedy's nearly fifty-year tenure as a powerful senator from Massachusetts. *Dang* it didn't look good for Warren. But don't fret, the seat opened up after Kennedy's death in late 2009, so while Brown was an incumbent he had only held the office for about two years.

Decades earlier, Brown had posed in the buff for *Cosmopolitan* magazine's Sexiest Man Alive centerfold—*come on, doggone it,* no woman politician could ever get away with that and be taken seriously! But the Big Money bosses were ready to be his sugar daddies. They would flood his coffers, making him a formidable candidate to beat. Running for office takes a lot of money, and the race ended up being the most expensive in Massachusetts history—in fact, the only election that year that was more expensive was the presidential race between Barack Obama and Mitt Romney.

At her speech at the Democratic National Convention, the new senatorial candidate Warren was charming, warm, and cuddly fuzz as usual, and from the looks of her always-flawless skin, ingenious oval glasses, and the humility with which she approached the sizeable mic, it could be easy to underestimate the academic in the house. These guys knew Warren well enough since way back for her sweeping fight for the middle class, and most recently, her journey with Obama to clean up the ash of the 2008 economic collapse, and they trusted that she was a fist that pulled hard for what she wanted. But they didn't know yet what it was to see her run for Senate; Warren could pull her queen cape on so quick it was almost blinding. They'd have to shield their eyes from the glow, baby. Warren was at the DNC to make a case for herself and for Obama's candidacy, so she served badass like birthday cake. Her speech showed that she could be a confident, targeted, and stern senator.

I'm Elizabeth Warren, and this is my first Democratic Convention. Never thought I'd run for Senate. And I sure never dreamed that I'd get to be the warm-up act for President Bill Clinton—an amazing man, who had the good sense to marry one of the coolest women on the planet. I want to give a special shout-out to the Massachusetts delegation. I'm counting on you to help me win and to help President Obama win.

And Mitt Romney? He wants to give tax cuts to millionaires and billionaires. But for middle-class families who are hanging on by their fingernails? His plans will hammer them with a new tax hike of up to 2,000 dollars. Mitt Romney wants to give billions in breaks to big corporations—but he and Paul Ryan would pulverize financial reform, voucherize Medicare, and vaporize Obamacare.

The Republican vision is clear: "I've got mine, the rest of you are on your own." Republicans say they don't believe in government. Sure they do. They believe in government to help themselves and their powerful friends. After all, Mitt Romney's the guy who said corporations are people.

No, Governor Romney, corporations are not people. People have hearts, they have kids, they get jobs, they get sick, they cry, they dance. They live, they love, and they die. And that matters. That matters because we don't run this country for corporations, we run it for people. And that's why we need Barack Obama . . .

By the way, just a few weeks ago, [the CFPB] caught one of the biggest credit card companies cheating its customers and made it give people back every penny it took, plus millions of dollars in fines. That's what happens when you have a president on the side of the middle class.

Warren could break down the situation, get to the heart of the matter, and serve the *tea*, dinner, and dessert all at once because she had viewed her opponents' political moves herself from the kitchen as a regular citizen, albeit with a professorial looking glass. She'd had no need for a political seat, but had already zoomed in on the systems and men involved. She knew their strengths and weaknesses. And she always told it like it was. The Democratic Party, and beyond, learned quickly that she was still Warren, on the same mission for the middle class, and she'd work her same agenda, ride the same horse, in the Senate seat.

But there were challenges.

No woman had ever won a Senate race in Massachusetts. The state has a liberal reputation, but its traditional politics have long represented a blend of the liberal and moderately conservative. It's a state with a history of legendary leaders—like John Kerry and John F. Kennedy. Scott Brown himself had made it to office by winning against a woman in the 2010 special election. And for so long it had been a man's game in Massachusetts.

But they'd never seen Warren go for the throne.

Brown was an incumbent, which *oh Lord,* meant that he could use the significant resources of Senate campaign committees as well as the Senate itself to boost his name recognition and popularity. Though Senate congressional resources cannot be used for campaign purposes per se, a press conference to introduce a meaningful bill or the passage of legislation germane to the state can offer *opportunities* for candidates to associate themselves with good work that may *impress* voters in their district.

Sure, *that's* not intimidating at all . . . but that wouldn't stop *the Warren.*

Winning is a numbers game, sis, and a strategic approach

to getting votes is vital. And strategy was Warren's key strength. She brokered a deal with Brown early in the race. Karl Rove, an infamous Republican operative, had taken an interest in defending Brown in his race for senator. As the leader of a political action committee, Rove had resources and a different set of rules that governed his foray into the campaign. After the 2010 Citizens United decision in the US Supreme Court, forces were working to deregulate campaign finance law to allow unlimited corporate donations to a campaign. Rove was prepared to drop big dollars in favor of Brown. He ran negative ads against Warren that twisted the truth and even made up lies. Rove's independent group, Crossroads GPS, created ads flipping the script on Warren, selling messages that said that she was "too close to Big Business," and that she facilitated bank bailouts that caused the financial crisis and bailouts that paid big corporate bonuses to bank executives while the middle class suffered. *Huh, excuse me?* One of the ads closed, with "Tell Professor Warren we need jobs, not more bailouts and bigger government."

Sis, we *know* that ain't right! Meanwhile, Brown's top-ten contributors included six big banks and financial institutions!

Grrrr, dial up Bruce and Bailey, this Rove dude needs to take a seat!

Warren recognized the damage that this sort of obfuscation and confusion could do: Many people seemed more interested in the aspersions cast by negative ads than the truth.

But when Scott Brown began to criticize the work of third-party ads in campaigns, she saw a window to make a deal. Liz is a smart cookie. She told Brown publicly that if he promised to keep third-party ads out of the race, she would too. He agreed, and by doing that she leveled the playing field of her own candidacy.

Over the course of 2012, she was able to close the gap between her and her opponent in the polls by waging a grassroots campaign with the steam of a mighty engine, endlessly knocking on doors, attending small town-hall meetings and gatherings, traversing the state to meet as many people as she could. And Liz doesn't get tired. She hit the phones daily, asking potential donors for money, to build up enough resources to match the millions Brown already had in the bank. Fortunately, people had followed her work on bankruptcy reform and the CFPB. Everywhere she traveled, she heard stories about people who had played by the rules: they went to school, went on to college, searched for jobs constantly, and could find no ways to get ahead. People had heard about the way she had stood up to the banks, had fought for them even when she wasn't their elected representative.

That personal connection to the Massachusites was powerful! Hundreds of everyday, regular people volunteered to push her over the top. She did attract some big donors too, but small contributors were her bread and butter. With the support of so many people behind her, she went toe-to-toe with a handsome, male, big-money incumbent, and our girl won!

She's *that* queen.

SENATOR ELIZABETH WARREN was sworn into office in 2013 as the first woman senator in Massachusetts history!

In her speech, she broke down her objective, which was the same as it had always been: to teach and learn, and to create structural change. As a junior senator she was assigned to the Special Committee on Aging; the Banking, Housing, and Urban Affairs committee; and the Health, Education, Labor, and Pensions committee.

As a senator, her job isn't just to sit around passing bills all day long. In fact, it's rare that a senator's bills and legislation make it to the president's desk at all. One of Madam Senator's great accomplishments has been the influence that she has over her colleagues.

Though President Obama and Elizabeth Warren had supported each other for many years since their first introduction at Harvard, Senator Warren pushed back against the Obama administration when she needed to; for two years she fought to wipe clean the student loan debt of those defrauded by the for-profit school American Career Institute.

It amounted to a zero balance for 4,500 students in Massachusetts! It was a huge victory for those students to receive invoices that sparkled with a zero balance, debts cleared due to Warren speaking out on their behalf.

Warren doesn't back down, not even when it involves the people she likes. In the final days of Obama's presidency, Warren opposed the $6.3 billion 21st Century Cures Act the president had signed into law. The bill would provide new funding to medical research, which is an important area to Warren, and $1.8 billion would be tied to cancer research, and it authorized Congress to send $1 billion to states to fight the opioid crisis. But it also received a lot of support from pharmaceutical companies and bigwigs in biotechnology and the medical-device industry. Everyone in Massachusetts was on board, or so it seemed—except for the lone Madam Senator. While others saw it as an effort to advance biomedical innovation in Massachusetts, Warren noticed that the final legislation had included changes that were seemingly only in the best interest of Big Pharma. They had "hijacked" the bill and packed it with "a bunch of special giveaways."

Hell to the no, thought Warren. "I know the difference between compromise and extortion," she said. Once again, our queen's top priority was looking out for the American people—even in the face of political victories.

Everyone knows that Madam Senator is like a mama bear when it comes to finances. And as a great senator, she never cared about what powerful people thought of her. Warren Buffett once begged her to be "less angry," but Madam Senator will call out liberal BS just as fast as the Republican kind. She doesn't have to try to win friends; she's influential because she operates like a queen on her own accord. There's nothing political about her friendships. She doesn't bow down or hand over her values.

And that's why she's a Queen of the Resistance. She is waging a battle against powerful interests that want big oil, big banks, big corporations, anyone with *big, big, big* and deep, deep, deep pockets. She refuses to let them have the last word on the future of our nation. The Warren is not having it! It's not the bigness that concerns her, necessarily; it's the fact they have disdain for the regular people who just want a fair shake, a chance to live decently and raise their families with dignity.

The fat cats are easy to go along with. For a long time, they've been able to pay for whatever it takes to win. But Sen. Elizabeth Warren is part of a new movement in American politics, run in part by women, dubbed progressives, who challenge the powers that be. She unravels the untruths for Americans that have led them to vote against their own interests. She's a sounding board, a roaring tiger not afraid to go out into the wild against anyone, anything, any politician or corporation who tries to take advantage of our share of the gold. She will hand-slap away the fat cats double-dipping in the pot, rendering the government a tool of oligarchy.

And make no mistake about it, she's a woman. Do with that what you will.

Snap. Snap. Double snap.

KENNEDY'S SEAT

It's hard to be a diamond in a rhinestone world.

—Dolly Parton, "Tennessee Homesick Blues"

The year 2015 was an eruption of many things that challenged government officials at the time to take stock of who they were as leaders, and where they stood on the issues that were bubbling and stirring unrest in the nation: racism, Trump, life's existence.

Elizabeth Warren already knew.

That year Warren gave a speech at the Edward M. Kennedy Institute for the United States Senate:

> *As the senior senator from Massachusetts, I have the great honor of sitting at Senator Kennedy's desk—right over there. The original, back in Washington, is a little more dented and scratched, but it has something very special in the drawer. Ted Kennedy carved his name in it. When I sit at my desk, sometimes when I'm waiting to speak or to*

vote, I open the drawer and run my thumb across his name. It reminds me of the high expectations of the people of Massachusetts, and I try, every day, to live up to the legacy he left behind.

In 2015 the nation had finally opened its eyes to the long history of African American deaths at the hands of the police, and it birthed what some referred to as the new Civil Rights movement. It was in 2013 when the nation watched the trial of George Zimmerman, a volunteer neighborhood watchman who shot and killed an unarmed seventeen-year-old, Trayvon Martin, in Florida. Martin was a kid on his way home from a 7-Eleven store, where he had just purchased an iced tea and a bag of Skittles. Zimmerman was found not guilty of second-degree murder and was acquitted of manslaughter. Outrage spread through the nation, and sisters like Alicia Garza, Patrisse Khan-Cullors, and Opal Tometi started sharing #BlackLivesMatter on social media, which went viral and lit the flame for a movement. Then in 2014 an unarmed eighteen-year-old, Michael Brown, in Ferguson, Missouri, was shot and killed by Officer Darren Wilson, who had fired twelve rounds. As the news made headlines, the pipe burst and the camel's back broke, and all of this community's generational pain slid right out onto the streets of Ferguson. Injustice met fire, and courageous activists led a charge for resistance. The city felt torn and bruised just like the hearts of those who had been affected physically, psychologically, financially, and culturally for so many years. Freedom rides were organized and #Black-LivesMatter led more than five hundred people from eighteen different cities across America to Ferguson. The Ferguson movement led to other protests in cities all around the nation and the world. The media exploded with images of people fighting back against the killing of Black men, there were T-shirts made, and television writers hammered out scripts and episodes with BLM as their theme. It was officially time to be *woke*. Then nine churchgoers were shot in Charleston, South Carolina, by a teenage white supremacist, and President Obama gave a eulogy for those killed in the brutal massacre. A bold activist, Bree Newsome, climbed a flagpole in a town just outside of Charleston and removed the Confederate flag, which led to more protests and tons and tons of debate. Apparently, there was another face of America that didn't agree with Black Lives Matter, a face that was white, that we had seen many times before in many forms and that would continue to haunt a nation whose schoolbooks told us that Abraham Lincoln changed. The white supremacists began to show up more and more frequently, and just like Black Lives Matter, they too had a voice on the internet.

America was under protest.

Obviously the nation's leaders running Congress had to pick a side. If you're like Warren in a state that can be a li'l blue, a li'l red, there's always a middle ground that politicians can run to, especially under cover of their politics-speak. But this "new Civil Rights movement" forced government officials to identify who they were. Were they going to step up? Warren has always known what she'd been striving for. When she battles for the middle class, she's talking about Black Americans too. When she stepped up to the mic that day at the Kennedy Institute (and has many days since), she's speaking about Black lives. From her viewpoint, as a policy and finance *boss*, her position is that we need to create change in the systems all around; there have been too many pitfalls in the apparatus of the government that have left African Americans by the wayside, that need to be sealed up and fixed once and for all. For example, Elizabeth Warren will boldly say in any room, at any time, on any day of the week that you may need to call her up, that she advocates for reparations for African Americans, and her sensei skills can back up and break down exactly why, like it's a martial art. It's the violence and it's also the chokehold of some government doings that continue to try to metaphorically handcuff African Americans with their faces buried in the ground, the very way the police have had a history of harming their bodies and incarcerating their lives. The violence is way beyond physical. It's also way beyond the numbers, and while Warren doesn't have all the answers to a country so deeply entrenched and bound in racist history, she does know the areas where she'd like to help bring forth change. She knows exactly who she is, and she spoke out about that in a 2015 speech at the Edward M. Kennedy Institute for the United States Senate:

> *We must be honest: Fifty years after John Kennedy and Martin Luther King Jr. spoke out, violence against African Americans has not disappeared.*
>
> *And what about voting rights? Two years ago, five conservative justices on the Supreme Court gutted the Voting Rights Act, opening the floodgates ever wider for measures designed to suppress minority voting. Today, the specific tools of oppression have changed: voter ID laws, racial gerrymandering, and mass disfranchisement through a criminal justice system that disproportionately incarcerates Black citizens. The tools have changed, but Black voters are still deliberately cut out of the political process.*
>
> *Violence. Voting. And what about economic injustice? Research shows that the legal changes in the Civil Rights era created new employment and housing opportunities. In the 1960s and the 1970s, African American men and women began to close the wage gap with white workers, giving millions of Black families hope that they might build real wealth.*
>
> *But then, Republicans' trickle-down economic theory arrived. Just as this country was taking the first steps to-*

ward economic justice, the Republicans pushed a theory that meant helping the richest people and the most powerful corporations get richer and more powerful. I'll just do one statistic on this: From 1980 to 2012, GDP continued to rise, but how much of the income growth went to the 90 percent of America—everyone outside the top 10 percent—Black, white, Latino? None. Zero. Nothing. One hundred percent of all the new income produced in this country over the past thirty years has gone to the top 10 percent.

Today, 90 percent of Americans see no real wage growth. For African Americans, who were so far behind earlier in the twentieth century, this means that since the 1980s they have been hit particularly hard. In January of this year, African American unemployment was 10.3 percent—more than twice the rate of white unemployment. And, after beginning to make progress during the Civil Rights era to close the wealth gap between Black and white families, in the 1980s the wealth gap exploded, so that from 1984 to 2009, the wealth gap between Black and white families tripled.

The 2008 housing collapse destroyed trillions in family wealth across the country, but the crash hit African Americans like a punch in the gut.

Warren sees the world like an economist, and for her the more we have control of the money and government, the more pressure we can apply in targeted areas that can result in change. Warren doesn't break down the numbers just to count the pennies; she's used them to tell a story about a long history that still has not been reckoned with by certain (a lot of) American voters.

And this ignorance is exactly what former reality-show host of *The Apprentice* Donald Trump leveraged to run for office.

And this is what it looked like: Enter Trump ››› enter chaos, more Trump ››› more chaos. **eye-roll**

In 2016, years after her first speech at the Democratic National Convention, Elizabeth Warren was a bigger star. She was asked almost daily if she'd run for president. To which she answered no almost daily. Her liberal colleagues, fans, and the media were advocating for her to run. She had just been through a Senate race, and wanted to get her footing in her job to deliver there. Plus, this DNC appearance was not about her, it was about her girl Hillary, who was running for president and who Elizabeth Warren felt would do good for the middle class. It was also about making sure that our nation—especially communities of color, LGBTQ people, immigrants, and Muslims—didn't have to deal with the racist, xenophobic, homophobic rhetoric Trump was spitting into the ears of his followers. Warren was the Dems' choice, second to Hillary, for who should run, and not all was lost, because Warren was one of the best weapons that Hillary could have. Hillary was smart but Warren knew how to fire back! "Trump's entire campaign is just one more late-night Trump infomercial. Hand over your money, your jobs, your children's future, and the Great Trump Hot Air Machine will reveal all the answers," she said. "And, for one low, low price, he'll even throw in a goofy hat."

Senator Warren was obviously voting for Hillary, and her message was that we should too. "We are here tonight because America faces a choice, the choice of a new president. On one side is a man who inherited a fortune from his father and kept it going by cheating people and skipping out on debts. A man who has never sacrificed anything for anyone. A man who cares only for himself—every minute of every day. On the other side is one of the smartest, toughest, most tenacious people on the planet—a woman who fights for children, for women, for healthcare, for human rights, a woman who fights for all of us, and who is strong enough to win . . . We're here today because our choice is Hillary Clinton! I'm with Hillary!"

Warren was a serious Hillary supporter, which meant she got into a lot of heated fights with Trump onstage and on Twitter—most of the them resulting in Trump being at a loss for words, cowering when confronted by her and trying to escape any issue that had arisen like a kid running home to Mama. The thing is, if he wanted to be a bully, Warren showed him that not everyone is afraid of bullies, especially when they were trying to do something as outrageous as run for president and throw around their power at any racist or homophobic bat boy who would fall for him. Their exchanges would go a little something like this:

> @ewarren: A thin-skinned bully who thinks humiliating women at 3am qualifies him to be President does not understand America & is not fit to lead.
>
> @realdonaldtrump: For those few people knocking me for tweeting at three o'clock in the morning, at least you know I will be there, awake, to answer the call!
>
> @ewarren: Is this what keeps you up at night, @realDonaldTrump? Thinking of new & interesting ways to call women fat or ugly or sluts?

Warren doesn't go around picking fights just because she knows how to. She prefers that things remain professional, congenial for the sake of getting the real work done. But he was acting disgusting on Twitter and the Queens of the Resistance just don't play dat shit. Warren's message was clear: Stop trying to act tough if you're not, bruh! Tough was

Elizabeth Warren, and please don't come for her if you can't handle it. Sadly, Trump would try to arrange comebacks like "she's sad to watch" or give her silly nicknames, but it all boiled down to the fact he was a sad communicator with really little to offer on the important stuff, and that just could not hold up against Warren; it was inevitable that he'd lose in any debate with this queen. One didn't need to be so smart to see that his darkness couldn't even come close to her light—girl, nobody wanted him to go blind!

Unless you've been living in a bunker two thousand meters below ground level in preparation for the end of the world, the 2016 election resulted in a tragic story that we've all heard before, where unfortunately Hillary did win more votes but was cheated out of her rightful throne. **eye-roll**

Honey, when Trump took office in 2017, we marched. Warren was right there in Boston marching along with us:

> *We're here today because of the power of women. The power of women to come up with good ideas like this rally. The power of women to organize like this rally. And the power of women to make sure that our country enters a new political era. That the voices of the people will be heard. Yesterday Donald Trump was sworn in as president. That sight is now burned into my eyes forever. And I hope that same is true for you because we will not forget,*

we do not want to forget. We will use that vision to make sure that we fight harder, we fight tougher, and we fight more passionately than ever.

But after the march, Warren was among the small group of women in the Senate that had to work with this man, one that had the mind to say things out loud like "grab them by the pussy." Ugh, imagine that for a colleague, just gross. Even though Sen. Warren is open to working across the aisle in Congress, she draws the line at rubber-stamping the appointments of people who would do wrong by most Americans. The first thirty days out of the gate, Trump proved that he was everything that Warren knew he would be, what she described after his election as "a racist bully" and "pathetic coward"! In his first hundred days, he continued to do a bunch of wacky things with his newfound power that would piss people off, like the Muslim travel ban, or making efforts to construct a wall on the southern US border and limit illegal immigration, "to give unemployed Americans an opportunity to fill good-paying jobs." Or so went the rhetoric of the white men in his camp who blamed immigrants for their anger. In the age of Trump, from her position, Warren played to win at every stage and at every opportunity so that his divisive cells wouldn't infiltrate into the American body. She did a lot of campaigning and fundraising on behalf of other Democrats. The country may have been under a divisive leadership, but never has Warren been wrapped up in the game of which side of the partisan divide a politician should stand on; her focus is always most about what's best for We, the People, and her successes as a senator in working with both Democrats and Republicans reflects that.

More on her achievements outside of the Senate chamber in a moment, but for now . . . it won't make it into history books, but she worked with GOP senator Chuck Grassley of Iowa to introduce legislation to make hearing aids available over-the-counter. And they got it done. Along with GOP senator Rob Portman of Ohio, she cosponsored the Smart Savings Act to increase federal employees' savings; she worked with Republican senator Shelley Moore Capito of West Virginia on an opioid bill; she worked with conservative John Cornyn of Texas to make it easier for veterans to obtain commercial driver's licenses. Can conservatives and progressives get anything done? Warren's philosophy falls in line with Biggie's: "*If you don't know, now you know.*"

Her dislike for Trump wasn't a prejudice against the GOP . . . it was just him. But, sis, once he took office, Warren knew that she had to at least feign some sort of peace with him, and she did in a public statement: "It's no secret that I didn't want to see Donald Trump win yesterday but the integrity of our democracy is more important than any individual election, and those of us who supported Hillary Clinton will respect this result. President-elect Trump promised to rebuild our economy for working people, and I offer to put aside our differences and work with him on that task." If Trump was going to step up and be a good president, then she would get behind him.

But then he didn't step up and be a good president.

NEVERTHELESS, SHE PERSISTED

Elizabeth,
She took the floor
Then she took a breath.
—Shaina Taub, "She Persisted"

There were many, many incidences over the course of Trump's campaign that made Warren and women all around the nation protest him. Besides embarrassing the nation in front of our friends around the world, the strange-haired reality star, "pussy-grabbing" candidate did gross things like invite Bill Clinton's accusers to sit in the family area of a debate with Hillary to rattle her nerves. It was all impossible circus behavior, from the campaign trail and right on into the White House, and it was especially galling for someone like Warren who liked to play fair and preferred to hash it out on the important legislative issues.

Then, once again, she found herself having to fight back against the new president and GOP during the confirmation of Jeff Sessions as Attorney General. Back in 1986 he had been rejected from being a federal judge. One of the reasons was a letter from Coretta Scott King to the Judiciary Committee. Now he was being nominated to head the Justice Department, which included overseeing Civil Rights laws. The letter said:

Thank you for allowing me this opportunity to express my strong opposition to the nomination of Jefferson Sessions for a federal district judgeship for the Southern District of Alabama. My longstanding commitment which I shared with my husband, Martin, to protect and enhance the rights of Black Americans, rights which include equal access to the democratic process, compels me to testify today.

Civil Rights leaders, including my husband and Albert Turner, have fought long and hard to achieve free and unfettered access to the ballot box. Mr. Sessions has used the awesome power of his office to chill the free exercise of the vote by Black citizens in the district he now seeks to serve as a federal judge. This simply cannot be allowed to happen. Mr. Sessions' conduct as U.S. Attorney, from his politically motivated voting fraud prosecutions to his indifference toward criminal violations of Civil Rights laws, indicates that he lacks the temperament, fairness and judgment to be a federal judge.

While reading it Majority Leader Mitch McConnell tried to muzzle Warren and get her off the Senate floor. His argument was that Warren had violated Rule XIX, which forbids demeaning another senator (in this case Sessions, who was both the Attorney General nominee and a member of the Senate). According to him the King letter was doing just that. According to the memes that spiraled online afterward, it was *truth*! "She Persisted" became a viral hashtag; bags and hats with the slogan were raced off to the printers; women were getting it tattooed on their bodies. Elizabeth Warren speaking out became a form of protest; women would not be silenced. Warren said to the committee, "I am surprised that the words of Coretta Scott King are not suitable for debate in the United States Senate." She was cut off by the chair, who said, "The Senator will take her seat." And the GOP would eat those words, because their attempt to silence Warren became a call to action for women around the nation about reproductive rights and domestic abuse, and added flame to the fire to fight back against the men who were trying to destroy women's freedom to act.

And Warren would not be stopped anyway, she went on social media and posted herself reading King's entire letter right outside of the Senate.

BUT WHAT REALLY drove Warren *bananas* was who this guy had nominated as secretary of education, Betsy DeVos. They both were named Betsy, but that's about all they had in common.

First of all, DeVos didn't hand in her ethics form like Obama's nominees did and the rest of the education secretaries before her. That precedent was in place so that the hearing committee would be able to review it beforehand, so they would have chances to ask questions about it in public. But DeVos had not followed the rules and had not handed in her homework! What teacher doesn't follow the rules?!

Second of all, she was never a teacher. Yikes!

And she'd never even taken out a student loan! Yikes! . . . *And* neither had her "fortunate" children, as she put it. She doesn't know jack squat about student loan applications, stress at the registrar's office, and what it's like to be dependent on these resources, which has been Elizabeth's stump speech her entire career. How did Betsy DeVos get this job? Imagine the rage Warren felt. We should wonder if Liz and her buddy Obama would meet up every so often to take a shot of tequila for comfort over how the meltdown of ethics were becoming so blurred in the White House. Liz must've cried to her team a thousand times: Whyyy?! And to think DeVos was nominated by a president who'd created a *fake* university! *Ahhhhhh!* Liz could pull her hair out. And she was not about to play nice with DeVos either. She was not going to stay quiet about how unqualified this woman was. Warren called her out on all of this at a Senate Committee on Health, Education, Labor, and Pensions (HELP) hearing in 2017.

Ironically, both women named Betsy were dressed in

SHE PERSISTED!
BOSTON WOMEN'S
FREE CHILD CARE!
RESIST! RESIST! RESIST!
DON'T TOUCH MY OVARIES
THE FU RE
FEM
RESPEC

purple blazers and spectacles that day, DeVos almost like a mirror opposite of Warren in every other way. Warren was like a crouching tiger, awaiting her time on the clock to slay. DeVos sat there pretending to be Elsa, frozen in smile, and almost speechless from the takedown that was whipped upon her. I mean, *what can one do when the Warren's coming for you!* DeVos just sat there squeamish and still as if holding her breath, trying to keep her smile to make up for her poor answers to Warren's drilling. And Warren was drilling her down hard, sis.

"Mrs. DeVos, do you have any direct experience in running a bank?" Warren asked.

"Senator, I do not."

"Have you ever managed or overseen a trillion-dollar loan program?"

"I have not."

"How about a billion-dollar loan program?"

"I have not."

"Okay, so you have no experience managing a program like this."

At this point, Warren is just looking deeply concerned about this woman's mental health. Why would she sign up for a job to manage a trillion-dollar budget that millions of students depended on to help them succeed? Warren then brought up DeVos's lack of experience with financial aid. She also asked about how she was going to handle this task in light of Donald Trump having created a fake university, which resulted in him paying $25 million to the students he cheated—how could the Trump administration protect against fraud and abuse at similar for-profit colleges under her leadership. How? What did she plan to do?

DeVos said, "If confirmed . . . I will certainly be very vigilant—"

"I'm asking how," interrupted Warren.

"The individuals with whom I work with within the department will ensure that federal monies are used properly and appropriately, and I will look forward to working with—"

"So you're going to *subcontract* making sure that what happened with universities that cheat students doesn't happen anymore?"

If we could all subcontract our jobs and still collect the paycheck, that would be nice, but it's just not what employees are hired to do! Jeez.

"No, I didn't say—" DeVos stuttered.

"You're going to hire someone else to do it?" asked Warren. And you know she just wanted to fly off and say, *Hey, crazy, that's not how this works!* But instead she said, "I just want to know what your ideas are for making sure we don't have problems with waste, fraud, and abuse."

DeVos attempted to sort of nod in agreement with Warren and started to say that she also wants to make sure we don't have problems with that, and if confirmed she'll work to make sure that we are addressing the issue. But Warren, clearly with a razor edge on this woman who once again didn't seem to do her homework, schooled her on the fact that there's already an entire group of rules that could take care of the problem with fraud and she'd just need to enforce them. Now, the question remained, *would* she enforce them? She asked DeVos if she was committed to doing that. The gainful-employment rule said that "career colleges" should not be given federal funds unless they could actually show that they were getting their students prepared for gainful employment. But DeVos would not say that she would enforce it; she kept saying that she would *review* it. Not the same thing, lady!

So, Warren had to shut it down and conclude, "I do not understand how you could not be sure about enforcing them. You know, swindlers and crooks are out there doing backflips when they hear answers like this. And if confirmed, you will be the cop on the beat, and if you can't confirm that you will use the tools that are already available to you in the Department of Education, then I don't see how you can be the secretary of education."

And though DeVos was confirmed, Warren didn't stop there. She started a website called DeVos Watch, which she launched publicly on CNN. It's an informative timeline of DeVos's every move, every nook and cranny of her missteps in her undeserved position. It includes what she has done since being nominated and all the wrong moves she makes, as well as all the times she's ignored the senator and her efforts to make it right. It was a Lipstick Alley tactic, putting all of her negligence on blast—and showed that DeVos was being watched by a complete badass.

With the website and other strategies, Warren's message to the White House continued to be on brand; she was not one to back down. The cabinet should watch their backs if Elizabeth Warren is on the scene, and even if she could not pull them out of those positions herself, she'd be there ringing the doorbell the moment they gave her an opportunity.

Another toxic nomination that Warren strongly opposed was Trump's perhaps worst judicial nominee. By late 2018 Brett Kavanaugh's Supreme Court confirmation was on the line because he had allegedly held down and sexually assaulted a young Dr. Christine Blasey Ford while boozy at a high school party. In confirmation hearings, Kavanaugh threw one of the most incredible nine-year-old's tantrum in court, or in politics, ever. "I like beer," he said almost ten times. "Do you?" And kinda denied blackouts. *What the . . . white privilege?* How could someone behave like that in court?! And a nominated Supreme Court justice? And on sexual assault allegations? In the midst of the Me Too movement? Warren delivered a speech on the Senate floor in October 2018 against the nomination of Brett Kavanaugh for US Supreme Court:

Mr. President, last week millions of people were glued to their screens as Dr. Christine Blasey Ford testified before the Senate Judiciary Committee. Dr. Ford's account of the most traumatic event of her life was harrowing. The pain of retelling this story was evident. And she did it for no personal gain whatsoever. In fact, her life has been turned upside down as a result of her decision to come forward. The courage she showed was remarkable. Dr. Ford's testimony was credible and compelling. I believe Dr. Ford.

Judge Kavanaugh's testimony was very different. He spent more than forty minutes ranting, raving, and peddling fact-free partisan conspiracy theories. And then he proceeded to insult senators, to scream at the people who had the nerve to question him. He evaded some questions, and gave obviously false answers to others. It was a performance that would have been right at home on talk radio, or in a Republican primary campaign, or at a Donald Trump rally. But it was delivered by a judge who is asking the United States Senate to confirm him to a lifetime appointment to a completely non-political position as the swing vote on the United States Supreme Court.

The shade in her delivery was incredible! She continued to outright call his nomination "a sham." Warren understood that it all came back to what she had been saying for years. It was less about Kavanaugh for the Republicans and more about the power they'd have with him as an ally in the Supreme Court to get the power they needed to move Big Money. "Judge Brett Kavanaugh's nomination to the highest court in our country is the result of a decades-long assault on our judiciary launched by billionaires and giant corporations who want to control every branch of government. For years, those wealthy and well-connected people have invested massive sums of money into shaping our courts to fit their liking. Working in partnership with their Republican buddies in Congress, they have executed a two-part campaign to capture our courts," she said. Warren saw it as a once-in-a-lifetime opportunity for the Republican Party to insert a flea into our highest court. It was clear that Kavanaugh would be a yes-man who toed the line.

> *When the Trump administration sought to block a young immigrant woman's right to access abortion care, Judge Kavanaugh sided with the government, claiming that allowing the woman—who had done everything necessary to obtain access to an abortion—should be further delayed in obtaining that care, a delay that would likely have prevented her from obtaining an abortion. And when religious organizations challenged the contraceptive care requirement of the Affordable Care Act, Judge Kavanaugh again opposed reproductive care, arguing that requiring religious non-profits to submit a simple form allowing them to opt out of providing*

contraceptive coverage but ensuring that their employees had access to that care was unconstitutional.

And her list went on and on about Kavanaugh landing on the wrong side of consumer protection, environmental safety, voting rights, and gun safety. And most interesting of all, "Oh, and when it comes to presidential power and the rule of law, Judge Kavanaugh believes that sitting presidents shouldn't be subjected to personal, civil, or criminal investigations while in office. That's very convenient for the current occupant of the Oval Office." It would be convenient for *any* president about to be investigated for impeachment.

A FIGHTER'S VISION

Is it worth it? Let me work it
I put my thing down, flip it and reverse it.
—Missy Elliott, "Work It"

Let's be clear about Senator Warren: she doesn't always play on the defensive. She is really fond of preparedness and prevention. For example, sometimes people wonder why the hell Elizabeth Warren is always talking about infrastructure or healthcare and all the important things that uphold the rock on which we stand. The thing is, she's just always ahead of the game.

Infrastructure is a key word that politicians talk about in their speeches that elicits a blank look and eyes-glazed-over reaction. *Uh-huh.* It's a death sentence for dinner party conversation. But it's an important part of public service, and it's always at the top of Senator Warren's mind, next to the moochers and cheats on Wall Street. And it's a good thing too.

Infrastructure keeps the American economy moving. It's the roads and subways that transport you to work, which is what gives you equal opportunity to take the job you want, and allows you to provide for your family. It's the bridges and traffic regulations that get your employees to work at your new company and allows you to pick the best hires, and not just who's in walking distance.

When we're able to go out and make money, then we do better as individuals and as a nation.

Therefore, infrastructure improvements benefit all Americans, not just the powerful few, so it's no surprise that not everyone cares about promoting it. Trump's first budget of his presidency included a $1.4 billion cut to investment in medical research. This elicited more than just an eye-roll from Senator Warren, and she set into action to stop it. Medical research is an important contributor to our economic infrastructure, and one that is vital for our existence. The funds put into medical research are how we find drugs, treatments, and cures for diseases and illnesses. Investment in medical research produces more jobs too.

This kind of thing is what pisses Senator Warren off the most. At a speech for the Carnegie Endowment for International Peace, she said, "Infrastructure is a basic example of why we have government at all." It takes care of the people who live here, but it's at the bottom of the government's priority list. In recent years, China has invested 9 percent of its GDP in infrastructure and Japan 5 percent. (*Your Pocky sticks dropped on the floor of the Tokyo Metro and you want to eat them? No problem. It's that clean!)* The United States, by comparison, invested 2.6 percent. (*Your pizza dropped on the floor of the MTA bus and you want to eat it? STOP, it's a health hazard!*) "China is building a future while America is in political quicksand," says Warren.

Warren's not pulling these ideas out of thin air. She has the data to back it up. She's done the research. The truth is, from 1930 to the 1970s, the United States GDP went up and wages for middle-class Americans increased. But from 1980 to 2012, there was basically no income growth for most of us. All the income growth went to the top 10 percent. What happened? Under Ronald Reagan, the government began to invest more into the wealthy under a philosophy that began in the Reagan era: when the kings and elitists at the top of the castle do well, resources will "trickle down" the food chain to the poor peasants. But it doesn't. It stays at the top.

It's bothersome when the froth is so hardened that it's stuck at the top of your cappuccino, so imagine the effects of these vital resources not trickling down to the people who need it. And the infrastructure that had sustained America during its boom was shot. According to Warren that's "a government that is only here to work for the rich and powerful," and that must change. Money could be invested in federal infrastructure that could build the literal and metaphorical roads and bridges to push Americans ahead.

Real-talk example: The 2014 water crisis in Flint, Michigan, probably could have been prevented with more money invested in infrastructure. Due to insufficient water treatment, lead leached from aging water pipes into the drinking water, exposing one hundred thousand people to lead contamination. It has led to a public health state of emergency, dozens of lawsuits, fifteen criminal indictments, and the resignation of an irresponsible governor. The majority of Flint's population is Black, and the water crisis there is a case study in government's careless treatment of minority populations and the gaps in our infrastructure.

As a senator, Warren has made it her job to take care of her constituents; she is invested in building their future, not tearing it apart. She helped to repair the Boston Harbor, seven bridges in Lowell, and sea walls in Scituate, and secured a million dollars in grants for firefighters for safety equipment. She helped secure $216 million for the dredging of Boston Harbor that will generate $2.7 billion in economic activity for New England. She put $400 million for improvements into Boston's transit system; $14.7 million in disaster relief for Massachusetts fishermen; and more than $184 million for military construction projects in Massachusetts.

When Trump's budget suggested taking money from medical research, which she suggested would "especially affect the people of Massachusetts," Warren got together with other senators and fought to have the cut rolled back. In fact, she reverse-engineered it to get an additional $2 billion invested in medical research in Massachusetts. Federal research helps us develop new drugs, our planet's ability to create clean-energy systems, and more. "Businesses, workers, families, and our earth does better when we have state-of-the-art infrastructure," says Warren in her direct, straightforward non-sugarcoated way. "It's a core element of building a stronger, more robust future."

WARREN IS NOT only thinking about the bridges and tunnels when it comes to infiltrating new systems. And she has never abandoned her concern for African Americans and the wealth gap that she mentioned in her 2015 speech around the time of the Black Lives Matter movement. In fact, she's one of the few politicians who have mapped the plan.

In America's city skylines, full of bright lights and glass ceilings and dizzying billion-dollar castles in the sky, we still think the sky's the limit for anyone. But Warren understands that for women and people of color to achieve equality and equity, a real catch-up game still needs to take place, and she's advocating that the lawmakers address it.

Here's a little background on how we got here: Black Americans who were brought to the "land of the free" in chains starting in 1619, and would continue to put hand to field, hammer to nail, and build this country without a thank-you or compensation, were freed in 1895. It was more than two hundred years of captivity and then Black people were sent out to live as "equal" citizens with no TLC from the government.

Much of what played out in policy and regulations made it hard for African Americans to "settle." Though Black and brown people would be spoon-fed the American dream and told of the land of possibility and achievement, things would be made tougher for them. Racist policies that ran through the veins of America would make it harder, policies such as redlining. Starting in the 1930s, the Federal Housing Administration (FHA) color-coded neighborhoods. The government marked predominately African American areas in red, and the FHA denied mortgages to prospective homebuyers in those areas. That policy, and other policies like it, led to huge disparities in wealth accumulation and individual net worth over time. African Americans were locked out of the grid, literally.

Elizabeth Warren's plan for housing is to make up for that loss so that Black and brown families can have an equal chance. Her bill, the American Housing and Economic Mobility Act, would give grants or assistance to first-time homebuyers or those who live or have lived in redlined areas. It would help people whose housing investments were destroyed due to the 2008 crash. It would invest in 3 million new affordable-housing units and create 1.5 million jobs. Rent would even go down by 10 percent.

Warren's efforts to improve access to housing are in line with her lifetime of helping the most vulnerable in the US economy. In the time since her own childhood in Oklahoma, her drive to help everyday Americans has stayed firmly rooted in her heart, and her understanding of structural inequality has only grown more sophisticated over the years. We salute a queen with a plan for economic justice!

★ ★ ★ ★ ★ ★ ★ ★ ★ ★ ★

QUEEN

I can do this adventure because we do it together.

—ELIZABETH WARREN, CNN INTERVIEW, SEPTEMBER 30, 2019

WE TRUST YOU, ELIZABETH!

Woke up feeling like I just might run for President.

—Lizzo, "Like a Girl"

When Senator Warren decided to run for president of the United States, it wasn't a decision made in a split second, and her husband wasn't the first person she asked. He was the last. In their few interviews with CNN, Elizabeth describes it as "a conversation that happened in bits and pieces when two people live together." Meaning, one night she'd be brushing her teeth and ask, "What's happening in our country?" through hard nylon bristles and small slurpy puddles of toothpaste. One night he'd be cooking the meatballs, his hands all mushy from onions and chopped-up meat, and he'd ask, "Where do you think we should be fighting back?" Pre-Trump, this may have definitely been a typical Bruce and Liz or politically minded family conversation, but now many Americans were spending much of their time after-hours doing the very same thing.

Not as many couples were having nights in front of *Jeopardy* without these big political issues swirling in their minds; the news cycle was running crazy every day, with more about Trump (which crowded out other news and information that could have been valuable to the public, *grrrr*) and his latest "Thing 1" and "Thing 2," as commentator Chris Hayes would say, sweeping the headlines. Americans were adjusting pretty quickly to the drama. Bruce and Liz weren't alone in talking about the country's fate while sipping Michelob Ultras and taking turns on Xbox.

Bruce knew that Elizabeth was talking to people about whether she should run for president or not. And of course there was some math involved in this equation. She asked her key people for three reasons why she *should* run for president and three reasons why she *should not*.

She saved Bruce for last in the polling. And when asked for his list of pros and cons, Bruce didn't answer. He only said, "If you don't run and Democrats lose, you'll feel guilty because that will mean there will be no one to fight for the people or the issues that you care about." She knew that he was right. *Oh Bruce*. It became clear to Warren that she could not not do it.

According to Bruce, "She's the best person to do the job."

It still wasn't an easy decision. Warren would never make such a serious decision easily; she'd spend late nights racking her brain, running over the numbers, and going over the research. She'd never go into a fight unarmed. If she ran, it would be a discerning decision, a practical and grounded one. She needed inward and outward proof to know if she was fit for the position.

She asked her trusted ally, her king, simply, "Am I ready?" That was the totality of it. They'd walked around Fresh Pond many times going over the effects a presidential run would have on their family and their life together. "Am I ready?" she repeated. But Bruce refused to answer the question. Finally after what was probably a ridiculous amount of walking at the sprightly pace Warren can go, he settled on, "You're going to do it anyway."

And she did. There were probably more walks around Fresh Pond, but the decision was made. She was going to run!

How did Warren know she would get the support? She *offered* support first.

She helped raise tons of money for her congressional members. In 2018, she personally called 172 Congress members to offer her help.

And then she met with sixty-one of them face-to-face.

Who. Does. That?

Sixty-one meetings to ask other people if they needed help, committing her to do more work on their behalf. And let's be clear, we know that she already had many other things to do as a senator; it's not like she was home on retirement sitting with Bruce knitting hibernation sweaters for the winter. *Why did she do this?* It wasn't because she liked hanging out with these 172 people after work. She was being strategic. She didn't need to be told how to win; in order to create change there was a huge need for the Congress to be in alignment with the president. Especially in light of what went down with Kavanaugh, she knew there would be tons of work to do moving forward. Warren needed to be as consistent, persistent, and courageous as she'd always been, and that meant taking matters into her own hands.

The day that she announced her campaign was New Year's Eve. She had a press conference with Bruce and Bailey, their golden retriever, by her side. When asked how he felt about it, Bruce said to a reporter, "We've been married a long time and it's always been an adventure, so this is just another one."

Senator Warren never wanted to run for president. She just believed in government, and Trump and the GOP weren't doing a good job. It was a job a woman deserved a fighting chance to do. The country was suffocating in the hands of the patriarchy and a president who viewed the landscape through rose-colored glasses of misogyny.

Bruce and Elizabeth then drove to a rally in Lawrence, Massachusetts, and Sen. Elizabeth Warren announced her presidential run. She launched a five-minute video of herself at home with her mint-green kitchen cabinets in the background, of her and the children in old family videos, of her at work surrounded by data, in the weeds of the community, all with a no-nonsense voiceover about "billionaires who wanted more of the pie." She outlined the Trump administration's racism, xenophobia, homophobia, and its dark path . . . and then the video ends with a Kenny G–esque melody.

Her colleagues were fine with her videos and that she announced her run for the presidency, but they had their own thoughts about her 'tude. They mansplained that her ideas were too big. She was thinking too much. "I've got a plan?"—what? She didn't need a plan, they thought; she just needed a "good smile" and a viral slogan. *I mean gosh, little lady, don't get so specific with your "planz."*

"That's not how you win," one colleague carefully explained to Warren. Hadn't she learned from Hillary? *Too smart, little lady, that means you'll lose.* And God forbid she wear a pantsuit! *Nooooooo.*

Elizabeth's a pragmatist, so she thought about their feedback . . . and she thought about it . . .

> *And I thought to myself, what do you think folks said to the abolitionists? "Too hard, give up now, America is never gonna change." What did they say just over a hundred years ago to the suffragists? "Too hard, give up now." What did they say to the early union organizers? "Too hard, give up now." What did they say to the foot soldiers in the Civil Rights movement? "Too hard, give up now." And just a decade ago, what did they say to the LGBTQ activists*

> *who wanted equal marriage? "Too hard, give up now." But they didn't give up, they got organized, they built a grass-roots movement, they persisted, and they changed the course of American history . . . Dream big. . . .*

And Elizabeth's work as a professor, a bankruptcy expert, the creator of an oversight bureau, and a US senator has all contributed to a bold platform that probably would have been unimaginable not long ago. She turned that around, and why couldn't she turn this around too? Just watch her.

BAILEY FOR FIRST DOG!

I feel love, I feel love
I feel love, I feel love
—Sam Smith, "I Feel Love"

Of course, Liz had a powerful new ally as she began her campaign for president . . . her dog! His name is Bailey Warren, and as of this writing there's a fan Twitter page @FirstDogBailey with over 25,000 followers, and the numbers continue to climb. His hashtags are #ReadyForBailey and #BaileyWarren. He's a cute golden retriever, but his real charm lies in his tweets about policy:

> Hi! I'm Bailey Warren. I like long walks, belly rubs, and financial regulations that hold billionaires and corporations accountable.

Or:

> Helping mom talk to some important people (voters not fat cats)

Hi! I'm Bailey Warren.
I like long walks, belly rubs,
and financial regulations that
hold billionaires and
corporations accountable.

And:

> Persist even if ur sleepy.

A favorite:

> Friend: “I want a treat, what do you want?”
>
> Me: “Economic and racial justice that also reverses climate change”

He appears on the campaign trail with his mama and takes plenty of selfies. Bruce sometimes brings him along when Mama hasn't been home in a while because she's campaigning, and will email her photos of him keeping Dad company, playing ball, or on the couch chillin'.

Years ago, Liz and Bruce had another golden retriever named Otis, who died of cancer in 2012, during an important time in Liz's life—five days before she was elected to the Senate. It was bittersweet. Otis had been the one thing that could calm any anxiety she had when the fight felt as tough as nails. She'd come home and sit down to pet Otis and then the world would seem okay again.

Bruce brought Bailey home as an anniversary gift in 2018. He's named after George Bailey, Jimmy Stewart's character in *It's a Wonderful Life,* which the couple watches every New Year's Eve.

Initially Liz protested getting a new dog; she was still grieving Otis, and with starting a demanding senatorial role, she worried about who was going to care for a new puppy—even walk him. They should just enjoy the pleasure of an empty nest. But Bruce made the executive decision. Bruce said, "'We're getting a dog,'" she recalled. "I started to recite the list [of reasons not to], and Bruce just smiled. 'The heart wants what the heart wants.'"

Bailey's presence and puppy love on the campaign trail beside Warren through it all has brought so much joy to not only Warren but to us all! Every strong leader should have a cute doggy by her side.

A QUEEN'S LAUNCH

Put it on everything that I will retire with the ring
And I will retire with the crown, yes!
—Nicki Minaj, "Moment 4 Life"

The sun has set but there are twenty thousand people *lit* in Manhattan's Washington Square Park! A city that has seen the best of subway rats, bedbugs, and creepy taxi drivers is swirling with excitement as thousands of New Yorkers, usually irritable and rude in a strange loving way, now peacefully stand side by side, elbow to elbow, iPhone to Samsung. Today, Elizabeth Warren has cometh.

Queen, it was epic; red, white, and blue shone bright from the American flag sternly held by the great white arches standing like sentries over the stage where the 2020 presidential candidate would be. "And now I give you Elizabeth Warren," said the announcer, and Dolly Parton's '80s anthem "9 to 5" rolled through the crowd, "*Tumble outta bed and I stumble to the kitchen, Pour myself a cup of ambition,*" and phones are held up, waiting to capture the very moment she entered. Yeaahhhhhh, the crowd cried. Warren appeared royal in a purple blazer, popped collar, with a smile as wide as joy could ever be imagined to stretch. She was giving us life from the moment we saw her, her heart open and arms out so wide it looked like she would set off in flight. And the sea of people erupted, rolling waves of applause. *Warren! Warren! Warren! Warren!* Her soft, sandy bangs blowing in the wind as she moved to the mic.

And before she could speak, *Warren! Warren! Warren! Warren!*

She has arrived.

"Helloooo, New York!" she hollered.

"I am especially glad to be here in Washington Square Park. I've wanted to give this speech right here, not because of the arch behind me or the president that this square is named for. Nope. We are not here today because of famous arches or famous men. In fact, we're not here because of men at all. We're here because of some hardworking women."

On the campaign trail, Warren's become a queen at giving us truth, and the kind that will equally expand our minds and hearts.

She went on to tell the story of the fire in New York's Triangle Shirtwaist Factory on March 25, 1911, when New Yorkers found themselves stunned by a gigantic fire that had started on the top three floors of the building, and swept across it like a speeding bullet. The factory workers inside were predominately women, immigrant Jews and Italians who were working for $5 a week, and they wrestled against the fire for their lives. Many of them jumped from the windows, and as Warren describes it, body upon body hit the ground one after another until there was a pile of dead bodies on the sidewalk. And there were women trapped inside too. Piles of them later found dead. The exit doors were locked. The fire department's ladder couldn't reach to the top floors. According to Warren, 146 people died in eighteen minutes. She said that for years the women had been working for longer hours and lesser pay but their demands for compensation and better conditions fell on deaf ears; the factory owners were getting rich and did not want to change things. Instead, they negotiated with the politicians and government to help their own cause, which was to continue to keep their pockets fat. This continues to be Warren's point about how the injustices and imbalances within our system can sometimes have cruel and devastating consequences. "They greased the state government so thoroughly that nothing changed. Business owners got richer. Politicians got more powerful. And working people paid the price. Does any of this sound familiar?!" she shouted.

"Yeaahhhh!" her audience shouted back.

"Take any big problem that we have in America today, and you don't have to dig very deep to see the same system at work. Climate change, gun safety, healthcare—these three are totally different issues, but despite our being the strongest and wealthiest country in the history of the world, our democracy is paralyzed. And why? Because giant corporations have bought off our government."

On the campaign trail Warren tells it like she's seen it. In the 2020 Democratic debate in Las Vegas, she removed her guns from the holster they'd been tucked away in and obliterated candidate Michael Bloomberg in less than thirty seconds. "I'd like to talk about who we're running against: a billionaire who calls women 'fat broads' and 'horse-faced lesbians.' And no, I'm not talking about Donald Trump, I'm talking about Mayor Bloomberg."

Everyone at home watching was shocked, mouths agape. Oh snap! Twitter went crazy. Memes proliferated of Warren as an OG.

Bloomberg looked like he didn't know what was occurring before him, and there was no amount of money in the world that could get him beamed off of that stage, or we can probably guess he would have paid it right then. He was standing right next to her, staring straight ahead, as she laid all his dirt out into the public. *Oof,* was it a good *read,* honey. Warren had played it pretty cool and calm for most of the debates up until this point in February 2020. She'd kept the guns tucked away in their holster, but now with this plutocrat rising up in the polls, it was on. Dead on. And she was pulling out the brass knuckles. She'd been falling behind in the polls and she

PRESIDENTIAL DEBATE
IF YOU DON'T HAVE
A SEAT AT THE TABLE...

YOU'RE PROBABLY
ON THE
MENU

wasn't going to go out without a fight. It was time to really speak her mind. It was time for a comeback.

Viewers could tell that Bloomberg represented everything she couldn't stand about the current system of politics, and she planned to undo it. She wasn't about to stand there for the shenanigans and let Mr. Big Money confiscate our government with his multimillion-dollar campaign, not on her watch. Nope. As she said on that stage: "Democrats take a huge risk if we just substitute one arrogant billionaire for another. This country has worked for the rich for a long time and left everyone else in the dirt. It is time to have a president who will be on the side of working families and be willing to get out there and fight for them. That is why I am in this race, and that is how I will beat Donald Trump."

Candidate Warren, in any match, is always five thousand steps ahead of the other candidates. In fact, she took off the gloves and went swinging for all her rivals. While her rivals were resting in the wings, perhaps being fanned and feathered by billion-dollar leisure, she was making T-shirts that said I HAVE A PLAN, because she did. While everyone else was eating their granola and cornflakes, she got ahead and posted her plans online. She and her team were talking to advisers and experts around the country to polish their plans—they found a network of lawyers, economists, educators, medical and military experts, environmentalists, and more to help draft them. On top of all that, she'd been working on it as a citizen before she entered politics. Her colleagues?

According to Warren at that Las Vegas debate, "Mayor Buttigieg really has a slogan that was thought up by his consultant to paper over a thin version of a plan that would leave millions of people unable to afford their health care. It's not a plan, it's a PowerPoint. And Amy [Klobuchar's] plan is even less. It's like a Post-it note, 'Insert plan here.' Bernie . . . has a good start, but instead of expanding . . . his campaign relentlessly attacks everyone who asks a question or tries to fill in details about how to actually make this work. And then his own advisers say, yeah, probably won't happen anyway."

Suddenly she was like HR, laying out why these candidates were not qualified for the job. It was a brutal beatdown for all of them as she chain-sawed through their résumés and plans—calling out insufficiencies in word count and all (she noted that Klobuchar had two paragraphs, girl. **side-eye**). Elizabeth Warren was back, baby. And that debate put her on the map with many voters! Twitter and other social media blew up with new converts to the Warren campaign. Many voters hadn't paid much attention to her up until then, and now they were #TeamWarren.

Warren's campaign was based on transparency. She wanted voters to know exactly what she intended to do when in office. She doesn't suffer liars or BS well herself. In the Trump administration era, where everything seemed dark and hazy, she wanted to be clear with voters about her objectives. Big Tech, Big Money, Washington corruption, affordable housing, and student loan debt relief were the issues she was going in with, kicking butt! And she did rallies with John Legend and Jonathan Van Ness from the beginning of her campaign to show voters that it was going to be an intersectional and inclusive movement for all under her presidency.

Too many presidential candidates run for elections with just a vague overview of what they'd like to do once in office. They show some charisma and are associated with the right people (Biden), but their history is fuzzy and their plan is vague. Why is that? If most American employees are asked to do a presentation at their job, there's a fifty-minute PowerPoint presentation before the Q&A session.

With Warren, she knows her plan so well she can probably recite it blindfolded and after a fifteen-day flight in space. She can probably say it in both Japanese and Swahili backward.

These plans have become part of her DNA. They are her willpower, her fuel.

We know Warren, she probably would not have even entered into the race without having thought through plans for student loan debt cancellation, public land protection, the opioid crisis—major problems that needed to be addressed quickly. And if you have any questions, sis, she'll answer them.

★ ★ ★

IT'S BEEN SHOWN that Warren is a hard worker through all she's done at her Senate desk and in private with her campaign team, but selfies, according to Warren, are equally important. It may not be clear if Warren can twerk or dab, but selfies, she's got that covered. On the trail she became known for taking a crazy number of selfies. In her visit to New York, she took four hours' worth of selfies that day. OMG, sis, was there ice nearby? She must've been face-sore. Can one's face get swollen from smiling too much?

But she kept going!

She'll even retweet you.

(If you're reading this, it's #QueensOfTheResistance, thank you!)

And it wasn't just the selfie craze that made Warren our friend on the trail. Her speeches have a personal touch, telling the details of her family's struggles, whether it comes to finances or about her mother's struggle to believe in her dreams with her. Her warm touch was also new on the campaign trail. She even called small-dollar donors on the phone—wow, no one *calls* anymore—to say thank you, wow! And she posted videos of those calls on her social media too.

In Iowa it was reported by her campaign that she had taken her sixty-thousandth selfie. If you're not gunning to be a social-media influencer, the thought of taking so many may make you want to vomit, but her campaign is run by individual donors, and she spends most of her time embracing donors on all levels—her dedication built a real connection with her clan. Warren has always done what she needs to do to reach people. She did it back in the boardrooms of the Consumer Financial Protection Bureau, and she'll be just as dedicated to your Instagram.

On the selfie lines, her attendees were able to get a small glimpse of the real candidate at their level. They could pass her notes, give her real feedback on her plans, ask her specific questions that are personal to their needs. It was all face-to-face and heart-to-heart.

While during Hillary's run there were supportive groups like Pantsuit Nation, Warren was the face of her own movement. She was up front and right there talking and building a coalition for survival right with you in real time. What seemed like a simple Snapchat was wildly shared and connected her with her base; and even though she was the oldest woman to enter the 2020 presidential race, she connected with younger audiences.

The love trail was real. She's thoughtful and willing to relate to people in her speeches in ways many politicians haven't been willing to let themselves be as vulnerable to do. She's mastered the fine line of being politically informative yet approachable. While some candidates walk as if under a veil, she was the face of a daughter's Christmas cards to her family. She gave folks a touch of inspiration from a real human person on their level, and not just a face on television. In 2019, an Iowa student named Cameron Chisté presented a typical example of that inspiration in the caption of an Instagram post:

> Hi @elizabethwarren told me I was important tonight so catch me crying about that forever.

The selfies are more than photos, they will become family keepsakes and memorabilia of this remarkable time in history when women presidential runners have taken off.

A WOMAN IN THE WHITE HOUSE

When you are a *boss* woman like Elizabeth Warren and decide to conduct a major operation to infiltrate the patriarchy for the top seat in the Oval Office and cop the nameplate "Leader of the Free World," you have a plan. Unlike a certain other dumpster-fire president (**side-eye** you know who you are!), Warren knew that if she were to win, she'd have to move quickly, be ready, and start as soon as the votes rung in with victory; one or two terms could fly by in a blink. When Barack Obama arrived at the White House, he had a full dark head of hair and a sick hairline, and he left a silver fox but the hairline wasn't as tight; Michelle arrived a queen and, well, she left a queen. Sis, all of this is to say that time would wait for no one, but Warren knew that if she had a plan and moved in like the sensei scholar she was, she'd get what we needed done. And so, she prepared.

As mentioned previously, she sat down with her team, as well as experts in law, economics, science, and other fields, to create blueprints and plans connecting the dots in healthcare, environmentalism, Wall Street regulation, and more. There were drafts and rewrites, agreements, disagreements, and re-adjustments, but Warren had the lady parts (ahem, not balls) to map out how to resolve some of the toughest issues in the United States. And that type of due diligence and tenacity is why we need a woman in the White House. Not to hurt any good guy's feelings; there are some men who are mighty capable and more than some women, but since forever women have overall been getting shit done better—taking on corporate America, packing snacks, planning brunches, you name it, and all the while being paid less and recognized less. Yes, ma'am, it's about time we took on the task of whipping America into shape. This land is our land too.

Hail to the tribe, Elizabeth Warren was taking the United States to task.

She planned the policies and legislation that she'd enact as president, including giving every child a strong start from the cradle, and strong support in education all the way through to entering the workforce. **happy dance**

First of all, to all the parents and someday-parents, Warren planned to offer low- or no-cost childcare for ages zero to five, and when she says things like this, for anyone who has had to shop for affordable daycare it sounds like a cheerful lullaby and end to suffering. Unfortunately, too many families are challenged with whether to take a job or put their kid in a daycare with a facility so underfunded that the walls look like they may reach out and snatch the child.

It's that or the alternative, a place with all the zeros behind the dollar sign.

Childcare has become almost impossible for many families, and Warren has a plan for that. For past generations, free childcare sounded like a kind of magic that only Mary Poppins could bring about; it wasn't realistic. Warren will never forget the years when her babies, Amelia and Alexander, were young and how much of a necessity childcare was to her and how hard it was to find. She wants to give assistance to families because without it herself, she may not have had the fighting chance to become Elizabeth Warren the presidential nominee.

Warren's plan makes childcare an option to low-income and middle-class families everywhere in the nation, and ladies, that financial assistance would come from the government—not from having to stand in your nineteen-year-old cousin's driveway pleading for your life and begging and bartering services.

Depending on one's location, childcare costs anywhere from 9 to 36 percent of a family's income. Now, sis, imagine the toll that takes on families that are single parents or low-income households. Factor that in with other living expenses, and where is the room to build for a future?

Some mothers choose to stay at home, but, girl, there is a big difference between them and the women who are forced to quit the workforce to avoid the financial strain of childcare. State-level free childcare programs suggest that women are more able to participate in the workforce with this assistance available to them. As Elizabeth learned: happy mom, happy life. Let's just say it was best for the kids if Mom had a fighting chance. And that's what Elizabeth Warren plans to give them.

Speaking of wealth-building, Warren was also thinking about the people taking care of those kids—who've largely been other women. Warren and her team have outlined how to raise the wages of preschool teachers and childcare workers in America. Childcare consists of 2 million caretakers taking care of 10 million children. That was an insane imbalance of numbers to the Warren team, and the compensation wasn't measuring up to the hard work. Preschool and daycare workers earned only one-third of what elementary school teachers earned (and that's not much)—on average about $10.82 per hour. Warren created a plan to tackle this issue as president by providing grants to cities, states, and nonprofit schools and local organizations "to create a network of childcare options that would be available for every family," and the federal government would front the cost of running those programs. And families earning a certain percentage under the poverty line would pay nothing for childcare, zero, *zilch*! And for families earning more, sis, their contribution would be capped at 7 percent of their income.

Still, there was the worry about what the quality of those daycares would look like. Parents were breaking bank to ensure their child's safety and a decent learning environment. Warren's plan would adjust the overall childcare standards, and worker compensation would be similar to elementary school.

And ladies, remember all that talk about student debt?

Warren created a plan to provide tuition-free school and released a $1.25 trillion education proposal. She wrote in a post on Medium, "Higher education opened a million doors for me. It's how the daughter of a janitor in a small town in Oklahoma got to become a teacher, a law school professor, a US Senator, and eventually, a candidate for President of the United States. Today, it's virtually impossible for a young person to find that kind of opportunity."

One of her biggest plans was to provide Americans with free college options and to immediately do something to get those buried in debt back on the ground and on a level playing field. Warren designed a plan to eliminate tuition at two-year colleges and four-year public universities through a federal partnership with the states where we "split the costs of tuition and fees and ensure that states maintain their current levels of funding on need-based financial aid and academic instruction." Seventeen states already offered tuition-free community colleges, so the idea was not far-fetched. Maryland offered free community college, and provided up to $5,000 in scholarships to in-state students from families earning less than $150,000 a year; other states with incentives like this included New York, Montana, Hawaii, West Virginia, Rhode Island, Oregon, and Nevada.

Our favorite president, Barack Obama, had proposed this kind of solution in 2015 and in his final State of the Union Address in 2017. Warren planned to put it into action all across the nation. She also planned to incorporate a loan-forgiveness program that would cancel up to $50,000 in student-loan debt for every borrower with a household income of less than $100,000.

Hello, Madam President, let's do this all. *Whoop-whoop!* **happy dance**

Warren proposes, "a person with household income of $130,000 gets $40,000 in cancellation, while a person with household income of $160,000 gets $30,000 in cancellation." And borrowers making over $250,000 would not qualify for forgiveness.

And wait for it . . . to help cover non-tuition fees like books, Warren's plan would expand Pell Grant funding by

$100 billion over the next ten years. Pell Grant funds can be used for tuition and fees, room and board, transportation, books, supplies, and more, and though students are appreciative, it can also feel like pennies matched up against the great big gigantic massive bill to attend the school. So, Warren proposed a big extension of the Pell program for low-income students.

And to double back on the wealth gap, she created a plan for a $50,000 billion fund for Historically Black Colleges and Universities!

Umph, and DeVos need not apply to Liz's White House; she would hire a former *teacher* as Secretary of Education, *thank you*.

Warren's plans reflected the research and the data that her team collected, and it was just as much about analysis as it was about her lived experience that education can change lives. She'd gone from a small town in Oklahoma to a Queen of the Resistance in Congress—and we could count on Liz because she was one of her own biggest motivations. She was one of us. "This is about opportunity, the opportunity for every one of our kids to get a first-rate education right here in America, every one of them. Opportunity, opportunity to get a good job, to start your own business, to become a farmer, opportunity to do what you wanna do. Opportunity. It may just be opportunity to live independently, to have some dignity in your life. Opportunity, opportunity for all of our kids."

She would also tackle healthcare, another reflection of the struggles her family suffered and the prevalence of illness she found to be a destabilizing factor for families who declare bankruptcy. "The squeeze on America's families started long before the election of Donald Trump, and I'm not running for president just to beat him. I'm running for president to fix what's broken in our economy and our democracy," she says about her plan for Medicare for All, a comprehensive healthcare system that would provide coverage to every single human being in our country.

Trump had tried to sabotage Obamacare, and as president, Elizabeth Warren planned to return the favor by repealing all his efforts. In her first 100 days she'd lower the cost of premium drugs that many people depend on, like insulin; she'd also drop the Medicare age to fifty, and every person in America would join a Medicare option for little or no cost. From the moment she stepped into the White House in her comfy ballet flats, the corrupt insurance and drug companies would have to run and scatter, because the Warren would be coming in to regulate.

Elizabeth's plan was the first healthcare plan from anyone in the primary, of course. And it was specific; she'd done her homework. It laid out the full cost of the new plan and how we'd pay for it. Warren's plan was to provide better coverage to more people for less money. "I spent a lifetime learning about families going broke from the high cost of health care.

When I'm president of the United States, I'm going to do everything in my power to make sure that never happens to another person again." Warren was not afraid to make such promises because she'd already started doing the work. Nevertheless, everyone questioned where she'd get all this money. She had been investigating this issue for years and knew how to connect the dots. She knew that by removing big insurance-company profits, excessive drug prices, and other bureaucratic issues with insurance companies and providers, we'd save money and that money could go to actual care. There was an $11 trillion healthcare profit expected over the next ten years, and Warren planned to change that to zero. Her plan would eliminate premiums, copays, deductibles, or out-of-network bills. That means Americans would be able to keep what has amounted to thousands of dollars from leaving their pockets annually in medical expenses.

According to Warren, Americans should be able to go to the doctor they want, and doctors should be able to treat any patient; and health decisions should not be up to insurance companies.

AND SHE HAS more plans. A little more than a year before Warren declared her run for president, Brett Kavanaugh's appointment to a lifetime position on the Supreme Court felt like a loss, a terrible jab, a stab in the back to women, survivors, and democracy. She could not let go of the nomination of Brett Kavanaugh, and she worried about the future of the Supreme Court. Warren's plan would allow misconduct investigations of federal judges to continue even if they are elevated to the Supreme Court. **happy dance** "We will rewrite the basic code of ethics for federal judges," she said in her speech in New York. "And we will appoint a whole new generation of judges with diverse backgrounds and a wide range of legal experiences. Judges who actually believe in fundamental principles like [the] rule of law, Civil Rights, and equal justice."

She would ban judges from deciding for themselves whether a conflict of interest compels them to recuse themselves. She planned to extend the Code of Conduct for federal judges—currently there is none for the high court. She would also of course get at their money, and prohibit them from receiving speaking fees and all-expenses-paid trips from third-party organizations. It's all fair in law and war, and Warren's plan was to ensure that justices lived up to their name.

But it's unfortunate how many men were getting grumpy about Elizabeth's plans.

For instance, she's clashed with Mark Zuckerberg, who implicitly challenged her to "go to the mat" in leaked audio of internal Facebook meetings, which *The Verge* uncovered in late 2019. He pulled out some fighting words for Warren: in that same leaked recording, he said, "I mean, if she gets elected president, I would bet that we will have a legal challenge, and I would bet that we will win the legal challenge. And does that still suck for us? Yeah."

Sure, what a bummer for him. How dare she question why Facebook, Instagram, and WhatsApp are all owned by the same conglomerate? So what if all of an individual's info could be bought at the stroke of a button, and our democracy proved to be in danger? "Today's big tech companies have too much power—too much power over our economy, our society, and our democracy," Warren wrote in her plans. "They've bulldozed competition, used our private information for profit." She also expressed disgust with Facebook's policy against fact-checking political ads.

Liz's mentality is not only to win, it's to never, ever quit. Everyone just thought she was a schoolteacher and a book nerd even while in the Senate. Suddenly she was a presidential front-runner. And what's this— she doesn't play timidly? Some of the men in power were mad. But did Warren care?

To prove her point, Warren ran a false ad on Facebook claiming that Zuckerberg had endorsed Donald Trump. Then she tweeted about it to prove how Facebook was contributing—whether wittingly or unwittingly—to the "disinformation-for-profit-machine." She wrote, "If Trump tries to lie in a TV ad, most networks will refuse to air it. But Facebook just cashes Trump's checks. Facebook already helped elect Donald Trump once. Now they're deliberately allowing a candidate to intentionally lie to the American people. It's time to hold Mark Zuckerberg accountable."

Accountability would be a big part of Elizabeth's plans. She would create the Corporate Executive Accountability Act to hold executives of large corporations criminally responsible when their companies committed crimes, harmed large numbers of Americans through civil violations, or repeatedly violated federal law. This included tech companies, Big Oil companies, and anyone else, honey.

"Corruption has put our planet at risk. Corruption has broken our economy. And corruption is breaking our democracy," Warren said at a rally in New York City. "I know what's broke, I've got a plan to fix it, and that's why I'm running for president of the United States."

And of course that includes her plans for Wall Street: to "overhaul private equity, restructure American capitalism, jail corporate executives, implement a lobbying tax, and get big money and donors out of politics." *Bwa-ha-ha!* "I am a capitalist," she said in an interview with CNBC, "but markets need to work for more than just the rich."

Elizabeth Warren's plans were focused on regulating, building better standards and stronger accountability consequences, and putting more funds into the more important areas that mattered and needed help, removing them from the 1 percent of America's pockets.

Her plans for climate change would put over $10 trillion

I'M FIGHTING
BACK!

into the economy and create 10 million new jobs. As senator, she was one of the original cosponsors of Alexandria Ocasio-Cortez's Green New Deal resolution, "which commits the United States to a ten-year mobilization to domestic net-zero emissions by 2030." And Warren had Green New Deal policies, and she has broken them down fully, honey.

She plans protections that "safeguard our air and water standards, such as the methane pollution rule to limit gas and oil projects from releasing harmful gases; decarbonize our electric sector by restoring the Clean Power Plan. To put limits on carbon pollution emitted from our power plants." She'll set "tough standards for vehicle emissions, protect tax credits for electric and alternative fuel vehicles and infrastructure, and put real dollars behind transitioning toward cleaner electric vehicles and building a 21st century transportation system."

She even proposed a Blue New Deal to protect oceans and inland waterways. According to Warren, the funds would be available for all of this, yes, because she'd also "reverse Trump's tax cuts for billionaires and giant corporations—to subsidize the transition to 100% clean energy."

Elizabeth's mantra on the campaign trail was (1) Dream Big, (2) Fight Hard, (3) And Win. She knew that with a plan anything can be accomplished.

Elizabeth Warren once said that we need "a politics of inclusion, not resentment. A politics of courage, not fear." Warren was initially reluctant to go into politics, but then she grew into one of the boldest and most courageous politicians of our time. She started the fight when no one was listening—especially not to a professor with no real political clout. But Betsy's life, times, and rise speak volumes about what can be achieved with the right people in the right places leading our democracy. Her story speaks volumes to the power of individuals, one woman at a time, and also the collective. If a girl from the Midwest can grow and grow and grow into a leader of the progressive movement, women's movement, and human rights, united we shall stand and accomplished we shall be. "We can build an America unlike an America of the past," she says. "We can build an America of the future. The America where every single human being has value and is valued." Like Elizabeth Warren, we will always persist.

And we thank her.

ACKNOWLEDGMENTS

Our agent, Johanna Castillo, at Writers House is a true queen of the resistance and must go at the top of our acknowledgments. Wow, she is the very definition of love, creativity, and strength. We absolutely would not have had this opportunity without her strong vision and ability to keep us in check to get it done. We adore and honor you, queen. You are a changemaker who made our lifelong dreams of being published authors come true. Anytime you call us to have tea in your kitchen, we'll be there ASAP.

Thank you to the wonderful team at Plume who believed in this four-book series to celebrate these Queens of the Resistance. Special acknowledgments, high fives, dabs, and e-hugs to our brilliant, kind, and badass queen editors, Jill Schwartzman and Marya Pasciuto, and to the Plume team, who kept up the strong sisterhood and encouragement through and through to get this project done! *Yes, we can!* Thank you to the queens: Amanda Walker, Jamie Knapp, Becky Odell, Katie Taylor, Caroline Payne, Leila Siddiqui, Tiffany Estreicher, Alice Dalrymple, LeeAnn Pemberton, Susan Schwartz, Dora Mak, and Kaitlin Kall—and two good-guy allies who need a special shout-out, the editor in chief John Parsley and the creative director Christopher Lin. To our publisher, Christine Ball, a strong woman and leader from the moment we met her, we especially love the army you've built and the work that you continue to innovate. Thank you!

THANK YOU, THANK YOU, THANK YOU (in all caps) to our beloved Ava Williams, our research assistant. You didn't know what you were getting yourself into, lol, but your positive vibes and hard work held it up the entire time from beginning to end. Thank you for your warm and patient spirit throughout the process.

THANK YOU, THANK YOU, THANK YOU (in all caps) to the talented Jonell Joshua for your beautiful images and being a creative who could make it through all the deadlines with precision. You're the best, girlfriend!

Krishan would like to give a big shout-out to her personal sister circle, the women in her life who took the lead in helping with Bleu on those daylong playdates: my sister, Dominique Marie Bell, Raven Brown-Walters, Renee Brown-Walters, Lenica Gomez, Zaira Vasco. Special thanks to my crew at WeInspire—JLove, Brea Baker, and Taylor Shaw—and also to my mentors who guide me, especially Adrienne Ingrum, who has been a wonderful fountain of knowledge and inspiration throughout my path. This is for my mom, a queen of the resistance from Brooklyn and the Bronx, New York, who left us too soon but whom I felt watching over me from heaven smiling; and her twin, my loving auntie Amina Samad, who always came over with love and hugs to help throughout the process—I love and cherish you both so very much. Thank you to my Xavier Bleu Jeune for being such an awesome growing boy. I love being #BleusMom. My favorite moment in this journey was when you said you wanted to be a "comedic author" (not to be confused with author, okay). I love you. And last but never least, thank you to my copilot, Brenda, for rockin' this out with me!

Brenda would like to thank her friends on Capitol Hill; without your passion and determination to fight legislatively and strategically in this hard time, our democracy might no longer exist. My struggle for you here was to incline this project toward a true representation of your sacrifice, intellect, and capability. To special friends who helped me hang in there: Kathryn Williams, Cheryl Johnson, Shashrina Thomas, Ingrid Gavin-Parks, Kim Ross, Michael Hagbourne, Joan Kelsey, and the DMV Quartet. Thanks to Bernard Demczuk for opening the Growlery at Giverny West whenever I needed quiet concentration. To the absolute best parents—the late Myrtle Bowers Davis and Robert Lee Davis—who instilled in me the highest integrity, the best education, and the richest experiences. To Rep. John Lewis, without whom my career in politics would never have been possible. Thank you for your unwavering faith in me and unyielding commitment to art, inspiration, creativity, justice, and peace.

Thanks to Speaker Nancy Pelosi, Chairwoman Maxine Waters, Sen. Elizabeth Warren, and Rep. Alexandria Ocasio-Cortez for your bright shining lives of public service. Krishan, Plume, and I can only hope that we have begun to return to you just a small part of what you sacrifice so much to give to us all. Hail the Queens of the Resistance.

To our readers, from our hearts to yours, *thank you, thank you, thank you* for celebrating the Queens of the Resistance series with us!

SOURCES

ABC News. "Transcript: Elizabeth Warren's Democratic Convention Speech." September 5, 2012.

Alter, Charlotte. "Inside Elizabeth Warren's Selfie Strategy." *Time*, September 23, 2019.

Bailey, Holly. "The Transformation of Elizabeth Warren." *The Philadelphia Inquirer*, October 20, 2019.

Barrett, Amanda. "Elizabeth Warren." *American Government*, ABC-CLIO, 2019.

Bazelon, Emily. "Elizabeth Warren Is Completely Serious." *The New York Times*, June 17, 2019.

Berman, Russell. "Congress Nears a Breakthrough on Medical Research Funding." *The Atlantic*, December 1, 2016.

Bierman, Noah. "Elizabeth Warren Took Down an Obama Nominee from Wall Street. Was It for Nothing?" *Los Angeles Times*, November 8, 2019.

Burke, Caroline. "Bruce Mann, Elizabeth Warren's Husband: 5 Fast Facts You Need to Know." Heavy.com, September 30, 2019.

Burns, Alexander. "Elizabeth Lost Her Dream Job but Gained a Path to 2020." *The New York Times*, September 21, 2019.

Carnegie Endowment for International Peace. "Elizabeth Warren on American Job Creation and Infrastructure." October 8, 2015.

Casey, Maura. "Elizabeth Warren: U.S. Senator from Modest Means and Fierce Financial Oversight; Antonia Felix Charts Warren's Life Story, Her Successes, Her Marriages and a Central Controversy." *The Washington Post*, August 30, 2018.

Catalyst. "Women in Government: Quick Take," Catalyst.org, December 9, 2019.

Clinton School of Public Service. Video, 55:16 http://www.clintonschoolspeakers.com/lecture/view/elizabeth-warren.

CNN. "Elizabeth Warren Fast Facts." July 3, 2019.

CNN. "Interview with Rep. Gerry Connolly (D-VA); Trump Trying to Find Out Whistleblower's Identity; Congress Subpoenas Rudy Giuliani; Elizabeth Warren and Husband Give Rare Joint Interview. Aired 6-7p ET," *Situation Room*, September 30, 2019.

DeCosta-Kilpa, Nik. "Elizabeth Warren Reveals Her Favorite Dunkin' Donuts Order." *The Boston Globe*, March 28, 2017.

———. "Elizabeth Warren's Campaign Sent Dinner to Bernie Sanders Staffers After His Heart Procedure." *The Boston Globe*, October 3, 2019.

———. "Read the Transcript of Elizabeth Warren's Big Foreign Policy Speech." *The Boston Globe*, November 29, 2018.

Drabold, Will. "Read Elizabeth Warren's Anti-Trump Speech at the Democratic Convention." *Time*, July 26, 2016.

Economist. "Elizabeth Warren's Many Plans Would Reshape American Capitalism." October 24, 2019, https://www.economist.com/briefing/2019/10/24/elizabeth-warrens-many-plans-would-reshape-american-capitalism.

Fairy God Boss. "Millennials vs. Baby Boomer." fairygodboss.com.

Flegenheimer, Matt. "Shutting Down Speech by Elizabeth Warren, G.O.P. Amplifies Her Message." *The New York Times,* February 8, 2017.

Fortier, Marc. "Elizabeth Warren Reveals What Kind of Beer She Was Drinking in Instagram Video." NBC10 Boston, January 2, 2019.

Gass, Nick. "Nancy Pelosi: Elizabeth Warren Doesn't Speak for the Democratic Party." *Politico,* July 1, 2015.

Grim, Ryan. "Alexandria Ocasio-Cortez on Why She Backed Bernie Sanders over Elizabeth Warren." *The Intercept,* October 21, 2019.

———. "Elizabeth Warren on Her Journey from Low-Information Voter." *The Intercept,* February 19, 2018.

Harvard Law School. "Elizabeth Warren's Academic Record at Harvard Law School." YouTube video, 4:44, October 15, 2018, https://www.youtube.com/watch?v=sFzmSI-Seek.

Haslett, Cheyenne. "Young Voter Asks Elizabeth Warren Emotional Question About Acceptance." ABC News, December 2, 2019.

Herndon, Astead W. "Elizabeth Warren's Higher Education Plan: Cancel Student Debt and Eliminate Tuition." *The New York Times,* April 22, 2019.

Igoe, Katherine J., and Ineye Komonibo. "Bruce Mann, Elizabeth Warren's Husband, Is Low-Key but Incredibly Supportive." *Marie Claire,* September 26, 2019.

Jacobson, Louis. "Critics Say Elizabeth Warren Lives in a '$5.4 Million Mansion.' " PolitiFact, October 29, 2014.

Johnson, Rebecca. "Held to Account." *Vogue,* January 1, 2011.

Kang, Inyoung. "How Elizabeth Warren Responded to Mark Zuckerberg's Criticism." *The New York Times,* October 2, 2019.

Kaplan, Thomas. "Elizabeth Warren's Big Challenge: Winning Black Voters." *The New York Times,* October 6, 2019.

Kolhatkar, Sheelah. "In the Ring." *The New Yorker*, June 24, 2019.

Kreisler, Harry. "Talking to Elizabeth Warren." *CounterPunch*, May 2, 2010.

Kroll, Andy. "Why Is Elizabeth Warren So Hard to Love?" *Boston Magazine*, April 2, 2017.

Kruse, Michael. "The 2008 Class That Explains Elizabeth Warren's Style." *Politico*, June 25, 2019.

Lah, Kyung, and MJ Lee. "First on CNN: Democratic Rising Star Rep. Katie Porter Plans to Endorse Elizabeth Warren." CNN, October 24, 2019.

Lim, Naomi, and Joseph Simonson. "Elizabeth Warren Says She's Seen Enough Evidence to Convict Trump in Senate Impeachment Trial." *Washington Examiner*, October 4, 2019.

Lovelace, Berkeley Jr. "Elizabeth Warren 'Opened Up the Opportunity' for Us to Think About Breaking Up Facebook, Rep. Maxine Waters Says." CNBC News, October 23, 2019.

McCann, Erin. "Coretta Scott King's 1986 Statement to the Senate about Jeff Sessions." *The New York Times*, February 8, 2017.

McGrane, Victoria. "Five Things to Know About Elizabeth Warren's Record." *The Boston Globe*, November 2, 2018.

Morin, Rebecca. "Warren Hits Back at Facebook's Zuckerberg After He Criticized Her Plan to Break Up Tech." *USA Today*, October 1, 2019.

Moskowitz, Eric. "At Harvard Elizabeth Warren Has a Warm Reputation." *The Boston Globe*, October 14, 2012.

Newton, Casey. "Read the Full Transcript of Mark Zuckerberg's Leaked Internal Facebook Meetings." *The Verge*, October 1, 2019.

Nova, Annie. "Uber Drivers Block Traffic in Manhattan, Protesting Low Pay and Poor Working Conditions." CNBC, September 17, 2019.

O'Brien, Kathleen. "How Elizabeth Warren's Rutgers Roots Forged Her Future VP Prospects." NJ.com, June 25, 2016.

Olen, Helaine. "Elizabeth Warren Was Once a Republican. She Shouldn't Hide It." *The Washington Post,* April 16, 2019.

O'Malley, Julia. "The Rise and Fall of Sarah Palin: Plucked Away from Alaska, She Lost Her Soul." *The Guardian,* January 24, 2016.

Parker, Ashley. "Elizabeth Warren Emerges to Attack Donald Trump on Twitter." *The New York Times,* May 9, 2016.

Parker, Richard. "Why I Support Elizabeth Warren for President." *The Nation,* January 23, 2020.

Pierce, Charles P. "The Teacher." *Esquire,* May 1, 2014.

Plummer, Brad. "The Science of Global Warming Has Changed a Lot in 25 Years." *The Washington Post,* September 27, 2013.

R29 Editors. "Which Woman Running for President Is *Your* Candidate? We'll Tell You, Right Here." Refinery29.com, June 12, 2019.

Robertson, Adi. "Elizabeth Warren Says Facebook Has 'Repeatedly Fumbled' Its Responsibility to Democracy." *The Verge,* October 1, 2019.

Rubin, Gabriel T. "Kamala Harris Takes Aim at a Rising Elizabeth Warren." *The Wall Street Journal,* September 20, 2019.

Ruiz, Michelle. "Mark Zuckerberg: 'Fight' Elizabeth Warren at Your Peril." *Vogue,* October 1, 2019.

Samuels, Alex. "Elizabeth Warren and Julián Castro May Be Rivals—But They're Buddies, Too." *Texas Tribune,* October 29, 2019.

Saul, Stephanie. "The Education of Elizabeth Warren." *The New York Times,* August 25, 2019.

Scherer, Michael. "The New Sheriffs of Wall Street." *Time,* May 13, 2010.

Schor, Elana. "Elizabeth Warren Winning Voters on Campaign Trail with Personal Touch." *Business Insider,* May 10, 2019.

Schultz, Marissa. "'I Can't Afford an Apartment': Congressmen Sleeping in Offices Cry Poverty." *New York Post,* May 1, 2018.

Seelinger, Lani. "Elizabeth Warren Grills Betsy DeVos over College Tuition & Her Responses Will Worry You." *Bustle,* January 18, 2017.

Seelye, Katharine. "Elizabeth Warren, Known, and Maybe Feared, on National Stage." *The New York Times,* November 10, 2012.

Shalby, Colleen. "A Record Number of Women Are Running for Office. This Election Cycle, They Didn't Wait for an Invite." *Los Angeles Times,* October 10, 2018.

Smith, Allan. "Who's More Fit for Office? Democrats Work Out More on the Campaign Trail." NBC News, April 12, 2019.

Spencer, Tannis, and Alysa Lechner, "20 Ridiculous Rapper Mansions." Complex.com, February 27, 2013.

Stevens, Matt. "Elizabeth Warren's Immigration Plan Takes Aim at Trump-Era Abuses." *The New York Times,* July 11, 2019.

Tavernise, Sabrina. "How Elizabeth Warren Learned to Fight." *The New York Times,* June 24 2019.

Thompson, Alex. "Liz Was a Diehard Conservative." *Politico,* April 12, 2019.

Thompson, Alex, and Everett Burgess. "Warren and Bernie's Awkward Truce Faces Its Biggest Test Yet." *Politico,* July 30, 2019.

Thys, Fred. "When Warren Came to Harvard Law, the School Was in the Throes of Change." WBUR, October 31, 2019.

Toobin, Jeffrey. "The Professor." *The New Yorker,* September 10, 2012.

Traister, Rebecca. "Elizabeth Warren's Classroom Strategy." *New York,* August 6, 2019.

United States Senate Committee on Armed Services. "Subcommittees." Accessed February 3, 2020, https://www.armed-services.senate.gov/about/subcommittees.

United States Senate Committee on Banking, Housing, and Urban Affairs. "Subcommittees." Accessed February 3, 2020. https://www.banking.senate.gov/about/subcommittees.

Warren, Elizabeth. United States Senator for Massachusetts. "About Elizabeth." Accessed February 3, 2020, https://www.warren.senate.gov/about/about-elizabeth.

———. *A Fighting Chance*. New York: Metropolitan Books, 2014.

———. "Committee Assignments." Accessed February 3, 2020, https://www.warren.senate.gov/about/committee-assignments.

———. "Elizabeth Warren Addresses Racial Justice: 'Black Lives Matter, Black Citizens Matter, Black Families Matter.'" Speech Transcript, RealClearPolitics, September 28, 2015, https://www.realclearpolitics.com/video/2015/09/28/elizabeth_warren_addresses_racial_justice_black_lives_matter_black_citizens_matter_black_families_matter.html.

———. "Elizabeth Warren Speaks in New York City." Accessed March 22, 2020, https://elizabethwarren.com/nyc-speech.

———. "I'm Calling for Something Truly Transformational: Universal Free Public College and Cancellation of Student Loan Debt." *Medium*, April 22, 2019.

———. "Meet Elizabeth." Accessed February 3, 2020, https://elizabethwarren.com/meet-elizabeth.

———. "Misguided Data Freeze Keeps CFPB from Doing Its Job." *American Banker*, January 25, 2019.

———. "My First Term Plan for Reducing Health Care Costs in America and Transitioning to Medicare for All." *Medium*, November 15, 2019.

———. "Official Biography." Accessed February 3, 2020, https://www.warren.senate.gov/imo/media/doc/Official%20Bio%20with%20photo.pdf.

———. "Restoring Integrity and Competence to Government After Trump." https://elizabethwarren.com/plans/after-trump.

———. "Sen. Elizabeth Warren at Clinton College in Rock Hill, 9/28/19." https://scribie.com/blog/2019/10/sen-elizabeth-warren-at-clinton-college-in-rock-hill-9-28-19-transcripts2020.

———. "Senator Elizabeth Warren Questions Betsy DeVos at Senate Confirmation Hearing." C-SPAN, streamed live on January 17, 2017, YouTube video, 5:47, https://www.youtube.com/watch?v=ld6k2b-AEfU.

———. "Senator Elizabeth Warren's Speech on Racial Inequality in Full." *The Guardian*, September 28, 2015.

———. *This Fight Is Our Fight*. New York: Henry Holt and Company, 2017.

———. "University of Arkansas Clinton School of Public Service Speaker Series." University of Arkansas Clinton School of Public Service, streamed live on May 4, 2011.

———. "Warren Delivers Commencement Address at Morgan State University." Accessed February 3, 2020, https://www.warren.senate.gov/newsroom/press-releases/warren-delivers-commencement-address-at-morgan-state-university.

Weissman, Cale Guthrie. "Here's How Elizabeth Warren's Student Loan Debt Forgiveness Plan Would Work." *Fast Company*, April 22, 2019.

Young, Shannon. "Elizabeth Warren Touts Bill to Create 3 Million New Affordable Housing Units Across US." *Mass Live*, October 22, 2018.

Zhang, Jenny G. "What 2020 Democratic Presidential Candidates' Comfort Food Preferences Say About Them." *Eater*, June 19, 2019.

ABOUT THE AUTHORS

Brenda Jones is best known for her fifteen-year tenure as communications director for an icon of American politics, Rep. John Lewis. All of his published opinions, statements, and speeches, ranging from his introductions of US presidents to commencement addresses delivered to the Ivy League, and those celebrating his transformative Civil Rights legacy were penned by Brenda Jones during that time. She collaborated with him on his book, *Across That Bridge: A Vision for Change and the Future of America*, which won an NAACP Image Award. She has also worked in commercial television news and public broadcasting.

Krishan Trotman is an executive editor at Hachette Books, recently profiled in *Essence* magazine as one of the few African American publishing executives. She has committed more than fifteen years to publishing books by and about multicultural voices and social justice. Throughout her career as an editor she has proudly worked with leaders and trailblazers on this frontier, such as John Lewis, Stephanie Land, Malcolm Nance, Zerlina Maxwell, Mika Brzezinski, Al Roker, Ryan Serhant, and Lindy West.